the driving people

How your motorcycle works

Your guide to the
components & systems
of modern motorcycles

D1435146

C015312540

Also from Veloce Publishing –

Caring for your bicycle – How to maintain & repair your bicycle (Henshaw)
Caring for your car – How to maintain & service your car (Fry)
Caring for your scooter – How to maintain & service your 49cc to 125cc twist & go
    scooter (Fry)
Dogs on wheels – Travelling with your canine companion (Mort)
Electric Cars – The Future is Now! (Linde)
First aid for your car – Your expert guide to common problems & how to fix them (Collins)
How your car works – Your guide to the components & systems of modern cars,
    including hybrid & electric vehicles (Linde)
How your motorcycle works – Your guide to the components & systems of modern motorcycles
    (Henshaw)
Land Rover Series I-III – Your expert guide to common problems & how to fix them
    (Thurman)
Motorcycles – A first-time-buyer's guide (Henshaw)
Motorhomes – A first-time-buyer's guide (Fry)
Pass the MoT test! – How to check & prepare your car for the annual MoT test (Paxton)
Roads with a View – England's greatest views and how to find them by road
    (Corfield)
Roads with a View – Scotland's greatest views and how to find them by road
    (Corfield)
Roads with a View – Wales' greatest views and how to find them by road (Corfield)
Simple fixes for your car – How to do small jobs for yourself and save money (Collins)
Selling your car – How to make your car look great and how to sell it fast (Knight)
The Efficient Driver's Handbook – Your guide to fuel efficient driving techniques and car choice (Moss)
Walking the dog – Motorway walks for drivers and dogs (Rees)
Walking the dog in France – Motorway walks for drivers and dogs (Rees)

www.rac.co.uk
www.veloce.co.uk

This publication has been produced on behalf of RAC by Veloce Publishing Ltd.
The views and the opinions expressed by the author are entirely his own, and do
not necessarily reflect those of RAC.

First published in July 2012 by Veloce Publishing Limited, Veloce House,
Parkway Farm Business Park, Middle Farm Way, Poundbury, Dorchester, Dorset,
DT1 3AR, England. ISBN: 978-1-845844-94-3 UPC: 6-36847-04494-7

Fax 01305 250479/e-mail info@veloce.co.uk
web www.veloce.co.uk or www.velocebooks.com.

Readers with ideas for automotive books, or books on other transport or related hobby subjects, are invited to
write to the editorial director of Veloce Publishing at the above address.
British Library Cataloguing in Publication Data – A catalogue record for this book is available from the British
Library.
Typesetting, design and page make-up all by Veloce Publishing Ltd on Apple Mac.
Printed in India by Imprint Digital Ltd.

How your motorcycle works

Your guide to the components & systems of modern motorcycles

Peter Henshaw

Contents

Introduction & acknowledgments

The modern motorcycle is a triumph of affordable technology crammed into a very small space. Considering that it costs about half as much as an equivalent car (and let's compare like with like, because an ElectraGlide cannot be compared to a Ford Focus), this achievement really comes into focus.

Bikes have often lagged behind cars in their technology, but more recently they've done a lot of catching up, with features like ABS, traction control and digital fuel injection/ engine management all becoming commonplace on two wheels. It's a far cry from the motorcycling of a few decades ago, when intensive maintenance and roadside tinkering was all part of the experience. These days (chain drives apart) the average modern bike should not need any attention between servicing, though it's a wise rider who keeps a regular eye on tyre and brake pad wear, and oil level.

Despite all of these advances, many of the basic principles of how a motorcycle works are much the same as they were 50 or more years ago. This book aims to explain all of this in straightforward language and, when you've read it, hopefully you'll have a much better idea of what goes on under the fuel tank.

Ackowledgements
Thanks are due to all the manufacturers whose illustrations are used in this book: Honda UK, Kawasaki UK, Suzuki GB, Yamaha Motor UK, Triumph Motorcycles, BMW Motorrad UK, Harley-Davidson UK, Bosch, Cooper-Avon Tyres, and John Bristow of Castrol Lubricants (Retired). And to my brother, David, for the power/torque graph.

Peter Henshaw
Sherborne
Dorset

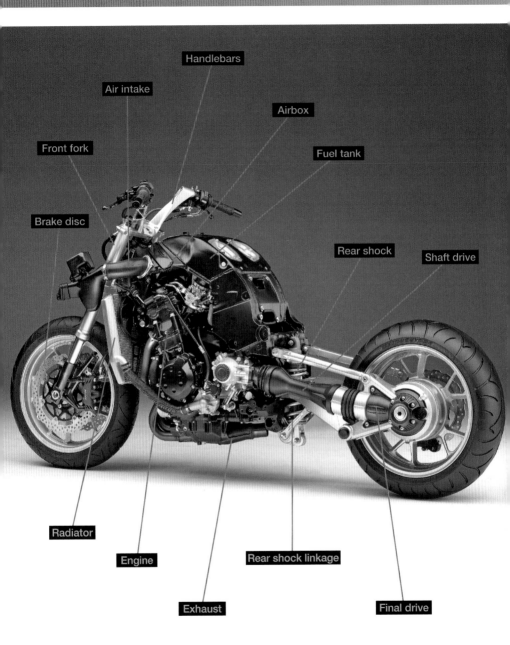

Handlebars

Air intake

Airbox

Front fork

Fuel tank

Brake disc

Rear shock

Shaft drive

Radiator

Engine

Rear shock linkage

Exhaust

Final drive

Anatomy of a modern motorcycle: 1 Brake disc, 2 Front fork, 3 Air intake, 4 Radiator, 5 Engine, 6 Airbox, 7 Fuel tank, 8 Rear shock, 9 Rear shock linkage, 10 Shaft drive, 11 Handlebars, 12 Exhaust, 13 Final drive. (Kawasaki)

one

Motorcycle types

Motorcycles are a diverse group of machines, which is part of what makes them so fascinating. The typical modern car has front-wheel drive and a four-cylinder engine – hence the high levels of advertising used by car manufacturers as they attempt to differentiate between very similar machines.

Types

Modern motorcycles may have one, two, three, four, or six cylinders, and come in almost every type of engine layout – they come as sports bikes, enduros or adventure tourers, aimed at very different uses and riders. Back in the 1970s, it looked like motorcycles were going the same way as cars, with the four-cylinder engine chain-drive layout becoming almost universal on larger capacity machines. Happily, they didn't, and today we have a vast range of different bikes to choose from, with disparate characters to match.

Naked bike
These used to be the standard roadster motorcycle, with no fairing, medium-height handlebars, and an exposed engine. Naked bikes come in all sizes, from 125cc commuters to 1000cc-plus muscle bikes, and what they offer is an undiluted motorcycling experience. They're cheaper than other types, and adaptable – it's often easier to fit luggage or other accessories to one of these. Also, the average age of riders is increasing, and a naked bike is the sort of machine many of them started on. Retro nakeds, like the Triumph Bonneville, deliberately evoke a bygone era.

Sports bike
Sports bikes are highly focussed on one thing – performance – with considerations such as comfort and

Naked bikes, such as this Triumph Bonneville, give an undiluted motorcycling experience. (Triumph)

Sports bikes like this Yamaha R1 have performance and handling as top priorities. (Yamaha)

practicality coming second. The lean-forward riding position and streamlined fairing mimic those of a racing bike, and, in fact, most sports bikes can be raced with only minimal modifications. Most sports bikes are either 600cc 'supersports' such as the Suzuki GSX-R600, or 1000cc-plus (Honda FireBlade, Yamaha R1). High insurance and running costs have blunted sales of the sports bike in recent years.

Sports tourer
The sports tourer is a sort of hybrid between a sports bike and a tourer, combining the best elements of both: a sporty riding position, with extra room for a pillion, and provision for luggage. Sports tourers are usually big-engined (at least 800cc) with excellent performance and handling, plus the ability to accept hard luggage. Many riders like sports tourers for their ability to be taken on a track day, as well as a two-up touring holiday.

Best of two worlds. Sports and touring bikes combine in this Triumph Sprint ST sports tourer. (Triumph)

Adventure tourer
Pioneered by BMW with the R80G/S, back in the 1980s, the adventure tourer is really the two-wheeled equivalent of a Range Rover – a big and well-equipped machine with a suggestion of off-road ability. The off-road ability is often nominal, though harder edged adventure tourers such as the KTM Adventure are capable of tackling the rough stuff. Sizes range from the 700cc Honda Transalp, to the 1200cc Triumph Explorer. Most adventure tourers, with their upright riding position and long travel suspension, are very comfortable.

Trail bike/enduro
These are genuine on/off road bikes, smaller and lighter than an adventure tourer, often with a

Adventure tourers, such as this Suzuki Vstrom 650, are very comfy, but off-road ability is sometimes only skin deep. (Suzuki)

single-cylinder engine ranging from 125cc up to 600cc. Slim, with zero weather protection, trail bikes have knobbly or semi-knobbly off-road tyres. Knobbly tyres have less grip on tarmac compared with pure road tyres, but they can make a good town bike. The more focused enduro is a less forgiving road bike, but has more off-road potential. Another variant is the supermoto, a trail bike/enduro with smaller road tyres and very good brakes.

Tourer
Touring bikes are big, luxury machines, built to travel long distances with great comfort.

Suzuki DRZ trail bike, here in Supermoto form. (Suzuki)

Yamaha FJR1300 is a well-equipped and comfy tourer. (Yamaha)

They usually come with a 1000cc-plus engine and are very well equipped with items like ABS, cruise control, heated grips, and hard luggage all as standard. Tourers are heavy with a long-wheelbase, so they don't handle as well as lighter bikes, but can be hustled along surprisingly quickly. Excellent weather protection from a large protective fairing and big screen is an essential element, as is shaft drive and a generous fuel tank for big miles between fill-ups.

Cruiser
Most major manufacturers build a cruiser of some sort, and most of these take their inspiration from a Harley-Davidson or Indian of the 1940s or '50s. The essential elements are a long-wheelbase, low seat, and high pulled back bars. A big engine isn't mandatory (125cc cruiser styled bikes are popular with learners), but most opt for a V-twin of at least 800cc, preferably a lot more. In terms of engine layout, Triumph is an exception, with its parallel-twin Thunderbird and Rocket III triple. There are subtle variations within the cruiser genre – custom, bagger, tourer and muscle-cruiser.

Long, low and mean – the Suzuki Intruder is a typical cruiser. (Suzuki)

two
Engine

The engine's job is to transform energy 'contained' in petrol into movement via pistons, crankshaft, gearbox, final drive and rear wheel. Almost all bikes use some form of internal combustion engine (so called because the fuel is burned inside the engine), and the basic principle is easy to understand. A fuel/air mixture is ignited and burns in the cylinder, creating pressure that pushes the piston down. The downward motion of the piston is converted into rotary motion by the crankshaft, and transferred to the gearbox.

Rotary engines (using a trochoid piston that goes around rather than up and down) have been tried in motorcycles, but ultimately without commercial success. Diesel engines, too, have been tried, but the Track T800 is currently the only diesel bike in production. Petrol-electric hybrids may be another possibility for the future, though, so far the only entrant is Piaggio's three-wheel MP-3 scooter.

Electric-only bikes are also starting to become available, albeit from only a few manufacturers. Otherwise, all motorcycles use a petrol-powered four-stoke or two-stroke engine – the four-stroke is dominant.

How a two-stroke works

The two-stroke engine is becoming less popular because of its poor

Water-cooled, single-cylinder two-stroke; simpler than a four-stroke. (Kawasaki)

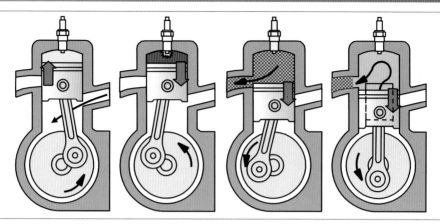

Two-stroke engine cycle. (Castrol Lubricants)

emissions, lower efficiency and shorter lifespan, compared with a four-stroke. But the two-stroke engine does have advantages, and is still used in mopeds, some small scooters and motorcycles, as well as smaller racing machines and off-road bikes. It is simpler, cheaper and lighter than a four-stroke, and produces more power for its size, with power delivered on every downward stroke of the piston – on a four-stroke, you only get a power stroke on every second downward stroke.

A two-stroke utilises what is known as total-loss lubrication: instead of a reservoir of oil, changed at regular intervals, two-stroke oil is mixed with the fuel, and is burnt along with it. As this fuel/oil/air mixture passes through the engine, it lubricates the crankshaft bearings, piston and cylinder bore.

Reed valves control two-stroke inlet and exhaust. (Yamaha)

The proportion of oil to petrol is very low in a modern engine using synthetic two-stroke oil. The oil is added to a separate, small oil tank, and the oil pump then adds the oil to the fuel in precise quantities. Specific two-stroke oil must be used, not the conventional oil intended for four-stroke engines.

A two-stroke uses the crankcase as part of the combustion process. As the piston rises, it creates lower pressure in the crankcase, drawing an air/fuel mixture into the crankcase. Meanwhile, the rising piston is also compressing a charge of air/fuel that entered the combustion chamber on the previous stroke. Near the top of the piston's stroke, the sparkplug ignites the air/fuel mixture, which burns rapidly, creating pressure that pushes the piston downward.

As the piston moves down, it uncovers the exhaust port, allowing the burnt gases to escape. At the same time, its downward movement is compressing the fresh charge in the crankcase, and it then uncovers the transfer port, allowing the fresh charge to rush through the port into the cylinder. The piston reaches the bottom of its stroke, and begins to move upward again, sealing off the transfer and exhaust ports as it goes, compressing the air/fuel in the cylinder, until it is ignited, and then the whole process starts again.

The two-stroke's perennial problem is that control of the gases is not as precise as in a four-stroke engine – some exhaust gases remain trapped in the cylinder, and some fresh unburnt fuel escapes into the exhaust pipe, reducing efficency and increasing emissions. Various solutions have been tried to overcome this drawback, with some degree of success. A reed valve or disc valve can control the intake/exhaust gases more precisely, Yamaha's YPVS system used rotary valves, and Aprilia developed the DITECH fuel-injection system. But in an increasingly efficiency- and emission-conscious world, the current two-stroke seems destined for specialist applications only.

How a four-stroke works

A four-stroke engine uses four strokes of the piston, rather than two, and

the four phases of the process are: Induction, Compression, Ignition, and Exhaust – also known as Suck, Squeeze, Bang, Blow!

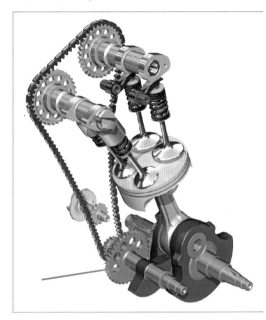

Typical DOHC single-cylinder engine, with four valves per cylinder and balancer shaft (arrowed). (BMW)

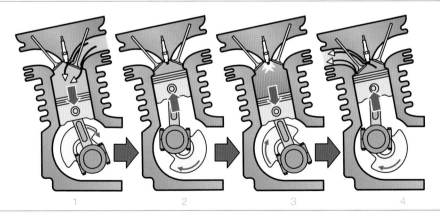

Four-stroke engine cycle: 1 Induction (Suck), 2 Compression (Squeeze), 3 Ignition (Bang), 4 Exhaust (Blow). (Castrol Lubricants)

As the piston descends, it draws in a fresh air/fuel mixture (Suck). At the bottom of the stroke, the inlet valve closes and the piston begins to rise, compressing the air/fuel mixture (Squeeze). Near the top of the stroke, the sparkplug ignites the compressed mixture, which rapidly burns, causing a very high pressure that pushes the piston down again – this is the power stroke (Bang). After reaching the bottom of the stroke, the piston starts moving upwards again, and the exhaust valve opens allowing the piston to push out the burnt gases (Blow). Then, the piston starts moving downward, the inlet valve opens, and the whole process starts again.

Put like that, it sounds quite laborious, but on a high-revving motorcycle engine these four strokes will be sucking, squeezing, banging and blowing many times per second.

The inlet and exhaust valves are opened by a camshaft, mounted above the valves (on almost all modern bikes) and driven by belt, gears or (most commonly) a chain directly from the crankshaft. A single overhead camshaft uses rockers to operate each valve, but most modern bikes now have double overhead camshafts (one for the inlet valves, one for the exhaust valves), doing away with the need for rockers – the weight of the rockers limits engine revs.

The valves are closed by springs, the exception being the Ducati desmodromic system, which closes the valve via a rocker rather than by spring pressure, giving better control at high engine speeds. Older bikes (mostly European and American pre-1970) used a pushrod system, with the camshaft mounted low in the engine and operating the valve via a metal pushrod.

Simple four-strokes, used in scooters and commuter bikes, have just two valves per cylinder – one inlet, one exhaust – but most bikes now have four

Single overhead camshaft (not in view) layout with rockers, arrowed, to operate valves. (Honda)

Pushrod operated valves are still used on a few engines. Pushrods arrowed. (Harley-Davidson)

valves per cylinder. There isn't much room inside the cylinder, but four smaller valves offer greater valve area than two larger ones. Greater valve area allows more air/fuel mixture to be drawn in per stroke, and therefore more power. Five valves per cylinder are used occasionally.

The precise timing at which the inlet and exhaust valves open and close – the valve timing – is vital to the efficient running of a four-stroke engine. In practice, the valves open earlier and close later than you might expect. This is because they need time to open, and the gases need time to enter and leave the cylinder. Valve timing determines the character of an engine: a high revving sports bike engine will keep the valves open for longer, with a longer 'overlap' (when all valves in a cylinder are open at the same time), helping to produce power at high engine speeds, but leading to poorer running at low speeds. Conversely, a low revving cruiser will have shorter valve opening times and a shorter overlap, which helps produce good torque at low engine speeds.

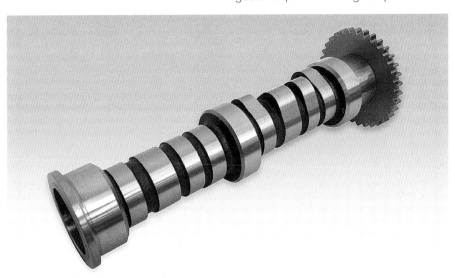

Camshaft for a parallel-twin engine. (Honda)

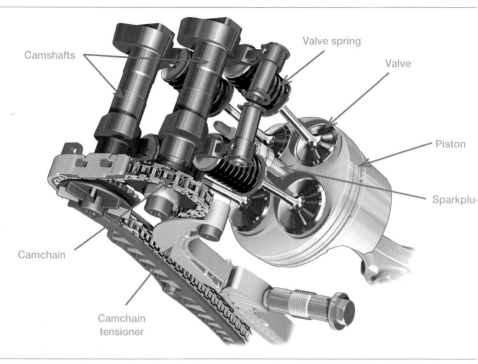

Camshafts

Valve spring

Valve

Piston

Sparkplug

Camchain

Camchain
tensioner

Typical cylinder head layout – double overhead camshafts and four valves per cylinder. (BMW)

Underside of a cylinder head, with space for five valves per cylinder. (Yamaha)

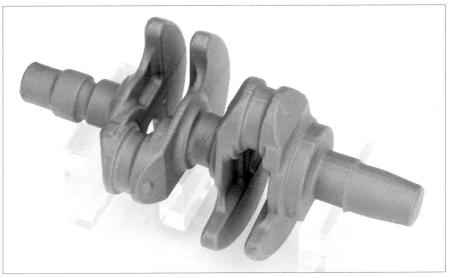

Unmachined forging of a 270-degree crankshaft for parallel-twin engine. (Honda)

Engine layouts

All of the previous descriptions assume a single cylinder, but this is just the simplest of a whole variety of engine layouts. As mentioned in the introduction to this book, the wide variety of motorcycle engines gives them all distinct characteristics and 'feel.' The layout that is used is often as much down to rider preference as suitability for the type of bike – some riders prefer the 'lumpy' feel of a single-cylinder or V-twin, others the high-revving urgency of a four.

What they all have to contend with, to a greater or lesser extent, is out-of-balance forces, or vibration. These are caused by the pistons whizzing up and down the cylinders many times per second, creating a pulse of vibration every time they stop at the top or bottom of the stroke, and start back the other way. Generally, the more cylinders an engine has, the smoother it is, because forces acting in different

Parallel-twin engine with two gear driven balancers. (Yamaha)

directions go some way to cancelling each other out, but there is always vibration of some sort.

Vibration can be minimised in a number of ways. These range from simple weights on the ends of the handlebars, to mounting the engine to

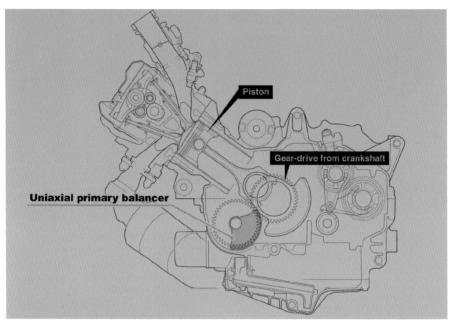

Piston

Gear-drive from crankshaft

Uniaxial primary balancer

Gear driven balancer for parallel-twin – the green area indicates the balance weight. (Honda)

Single-cylinder layout is compact. (BMW)

the frame on rubber blocks, which helps absorb the vibration. Many modern engines have a balance shaft within the crankcase that runs in the opposite direction to the crankshaft, and goes a long way to cancelling out those vibration forces.

Until the 1930s, most bikes outside the USA used single-cylinder engines, but demands for increased power and smoothness led to the development of multi-cylinder engines. The first of these was the V-twin, and it remains a very popular layout to this day, offering relatively good balance in a slim package. V-twins mounted in line with the frame (today only Moto Guzzi opts for a cross-frame V-twin) do take up a lot of space, especially with a 90 degree angle between the cylinders (which is the best choice for balance).

The parallel-twin (sometimes called the vertical twin) is another popular layout, though less so in recent times. Forever associated with older British bikes, such as Triumph, BSA, and Norton, it consists of two cylinders side-by-side. The pistons may go up and down at the same time (a 360 degree twin), or up and down alternately (180 degree twin). Both types have their own vibration problems.

Better balance is offered by the horizontally-opposed twin, also known as the 'boxer' or 'flat' twin, in which the pistons move in opposite directions,

V-twin is a popular layout. (Harley-Davidson)

Parallel-twin engine. (Honda)

21

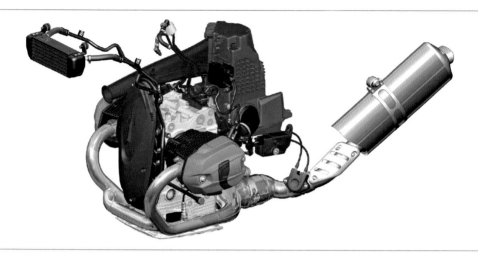

Flat-twin layouts offer good balance. (BMW)

thus cancelling out the main out-of-balance forces. Flat-twins will always be associated with BMW, which has been using them since the 1920s. With a crankshaft in line with the bike, they are ideally suited to shaft drive.

The in-line three-cylinder engine, or 'triple,' can be seen as a good compromise between a parallel twin and an in-line four, being smoother than the former and less wide than the latter. It can come with a 120-, 180- or 360- degree crankshaft, and in power delivery is a cross between the low-revving nature of a twin and the peakier, high-revving four-cylinder. BMW had its own variation on the triple, mounting one horizontally, and in line with the frame, in the K75 of the 1980s.

The in-line four-cylinder was arguably the standard large motorcycle engine layout from the 1970s onwards, and it's easy to see why. Balance is good, apart from a little high frequency vibration, and although width is greater than in engines with fewer cylinders, it's still acceptable for most riders. Four cylinders mean higher revs (and thus

In-line four-cylinder engine: still a popular layout for big bikes. (Kawasaki)

more power) than a twin- or three-cylinder engine of the same capacity. Variations on the theme have been the horizontally mounted in-line four on the BMW K100, the flat-four of the early Honda Goldwing, and the V4 popularised by Honda on the VFR range.

Racing bikes have used more

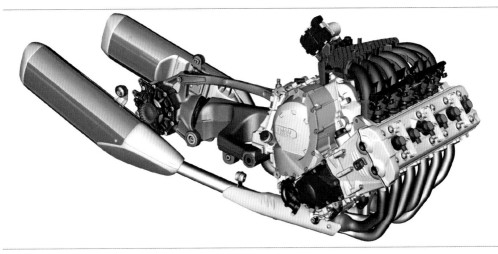

The inline-six is a very smooth engine. (BMW)

exotic engine layouts, such as a V3 two-stroke, V5 four-stroke (both Honda), and square-four (Suzuki), but six cylinders aren't unknown in a production motorcycle. The current Honda Goldwing, with a very smooth flat-six, is the obvious example, while in-line sixes from Honda and Kawasaki in the 1970s, showed the limitations of width. Recently, the narrow-angle V6 from Horex has made its debut. As for V8 engines (leaving aside the monstrous Chevrolet-engined Boss Hoss), there have been a few attempts to produce V8 motorcycles for the road (Morbidelli, Norton Nemesis) but none have reached production.

Power or torque?

A lot of confusion surrounds the concepts of power and torque. Some believe torque is produced at low revs

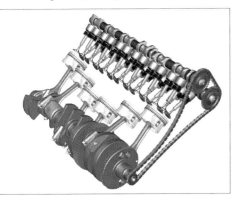

Six-cylinder engines offer great smoothness, but are complex. (BMW)

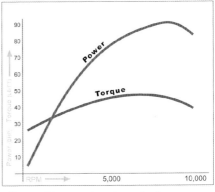

Torque (blue curve) peaks earlier than power (red curve).

23

and power at high revs. However, an engine produces both of them all the time, and the two are closely related. Power is torque multiplied by revs.

Torque is 'turning effort,' or the force that attempts to make something turn. When tightening a bolt, or unscrewing a peanut butter jar lid, you are exerting torque. So, in engine terms, torque is the force with which the crankshaft is being turned by the piston (or pistons) via the connecting rods. Power, on the other hand, can be described as torque over time – the mechanical energy the engine can provide over a unit of time.

Power and torque curves illustrate clearly how this works. A torque curve shows that, up to a certain point, the torque output increases with revs, then levels out and begins to fall as the engine revs rise further. Power, being torque multiplied by revs, continues to climb with engine speed, reaching a peak at high revs before rapidly dropping off as the engine over revs. The shape of these curves, especially the torque curve, gives a good idea of how the engine will perform. If the torque curve is 'peaky,' rising to a peak then rapidly falling as revs rise, the engine will need a lot of revs and gearchanging to perform well. If the torque curve is more gradual, it's described as 'fat' or 'flat,' and is able to sustain good acceleration in a high gear at low to medium revs. In fact, the shape of the torque curve is more important than the peak torque figure.

The cooling system

We think of modern engines as being highly efficient, but by the standards of many other mechanical devices they are anything but. The combustion process involves very high temperatures, reaching 2000 degrees C or more inside the cylinder as the air/fuel mixture is burnt. But only around 30 per cent of that heat actually does useful work, and the rest has to go somewhere else. A cooling system is vital to dissipate surplus heat into the atmosphere as quickly as possible. There are two means of doing this: air cooling and water cooling.

Air cooling
The earliest motorcycles used air cooling, and it remains a common form of cooling on retro-style bikes, some big cruisers, 125cc commuters, and small scooters. Air cooling often gets significant help from oil cooling, using the lubricant as an additional coolant by providing an oil cooler. Air has some

Air-cooled, single-cylinder engine. (Suzuki)

advantages over water cooling, making for a simpler, lighter engine that will not freeze or boil over. Many riders actually prefer the traditional finned look of an air-cooled engine, and some retro bikes have fake air cooling fins and a cleverly disguised radiator.

The principle behind air cooling is that heat rapidly dissipates into cooler air, aided by airflow over the engine as the motorcycle moves forward. But this isn't enough, on its own, to draw away all the surplus heat, so air-cooled engines have a multiplicity of fins on the cylinder head and cylinder barrel to greatly increase the surface area available for cooling. This does the trick, though the fins have to be carefully designed to cope, especially around the cylinder head, which, on a four-stroke engine, absorbs about 80 per cent of the surplus heat.

If the air-cooled engine is hidden from the outside airflow, as on a scooter, a fan is added to force air over the engine. This has the advantage of matching the cooling to engine speed (and therefore cooling requirement) rather than road speed through the air, so it's more effective than simply having the engine stuck out in the breeze.

For all its classic looks and simplicity, air cooling does have some serious drawbacks. As a system, it's a bit hit and miss, forcing the engine to operate over a wide range of temperatures – it's far less effective on a really hot day than on a cold one, for example. A less consistent temperature control means less consistent control of power and emissions. It also means that the various engine components will expand and contract at different rates, so manufacturing tolerances have to be quite large. And it allows more mechanical noise, which, as noise regulations become ever more stringent, should not be ignored.

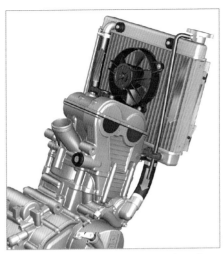

Hot coolant pumped, in this example, to the top of the radiator cools as it passes downward before returning to the engine. (BMW)

Liquid cooling

Liquid cooling addresses the problems associated with air cooling. Although it adds weight, cost and complexity, it does a better job of keeping the engine at an even temperature, whatever the weather. This allows for smaller manufacturing tolerances (which bring several side benefits), and enclosing the top end of the engine in a water jacket reduces noise significantly.

The radiator is typically mounted behind the front forks. (Kawasaki)

Cutaway shows coolant passages (arrowed) around a cylinder and in the cylinder head. (Kawasaki)

Cutaway shows a water pump (arrowed) driven off the end of the camshaft. (Honda)

Liquid cooling depends on a series of passages around the engine's cylinders and through the cylinder head (which takes about 70 per cent of the coolant, reflecting its higher temperature). Pipes deliver coolant back and forth between engine and radiator.

The radiator consists of two small tanks, connected by a number of small tubes, each one of which is surrounded on two sides by fins. The hot coolant passes through these tubes (either from top-to-bottom or side-to-side), and is cooled by the air flowing through the radiator. A water pump, often driven from the oil pump or camshaft, is fitted to keep the coolant circulating.

Since the whole system is largely dependent on air flowing through the radiator, an electric fan is fitted as well. If the coolant exceeds a certain temperature (for instance if the bike is sitting at a red light on a very hot day), the fan will switch on automatically, drawing air through the radiator until the coolant temperature falls again.

Another feature that makes liquid cooling effective, is that the whole system operates under pressure. The engine temperatures are such that water in the coolant would rapidly boil; adding pressure raises its boiling point.

The coolant is not pure water (hence the reference to liquid-, not water-cooling), but a 50/50 mixture of distilled water and ethylene glycol anti-freeze. Obviously, the system needs protection from freezing when parked up in cold weather, and as normal tap water contains impurities that would allow corrosion to take hold, anti-freeze also contains corrosion inhibitors.

Finally, there is such a thing as over-cooling, and this is what would happen if the entire cooling system was in operation when the engine started from cold. The engine would take a very long time to warm up, especially on a cold day, with uncertain performance and rapid wear, so a thermostat is fitted, a temperature sensitive valve that restricts the coolant circulation until the engine reaches a certain temperature.

Simple liquid coolant circuit. (Honda)

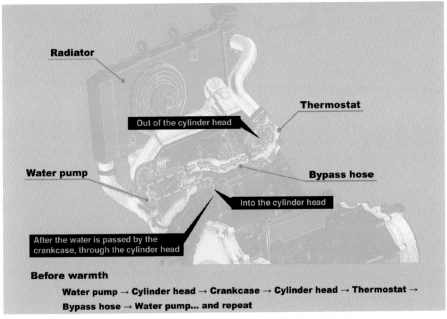

Before warmth

Water pump → Cylinder head → Crankcase → Cylinder head → Thermostat → Bypass hose → Water pump... and repeat

With the thermostat closed, coolant circulation is restricted ...

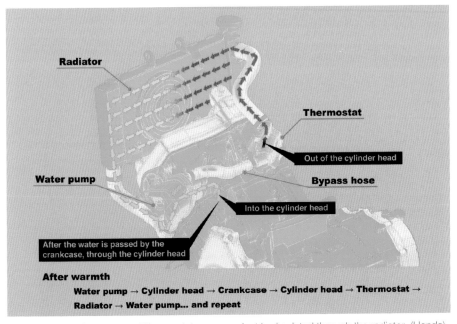

After warmth

Water pump → Cylinder head → Crankcase → Cylinder head → Thermostat → Radiator → Water pump... and repeat

... with the engine warm and thermostat open, coolant is circulated through the radiator. (Honda)

Lubrication

The finely machined surfaces of engine components, be they pistons, camshaft bearings or big-end shells, may look perfectly smooth to the naked eye, but look at them under a microscope, and you see a mountainous landscape of peaks and valleys. As components move past each other, the peaks of each surface clash, causing friction.

Friction is the enemy of all moving parts, as it resists movement and creates heat that will eventually cause the opposing peaks to weld together – this is what happens when a component seizes up. The only way to combat friction is through lubrication, which, in the case of a motorcycle engine, means oil.

Oil has several other important roles as well. Coating all the internal components, it protects them from corrosion. It also carries away microscopic particles of dirt, metal and sealant that would otherwise cause havoc between those finely machined moving parts. Oil improves the sealing performance between pistons and rings. In most modern four-stroke motorcycles, the engine oil also lubricates the primary drive and gearbox. And, as mentioned in the previous section, oil has a role in cooling the engine, often with the addition of an oil radiator, or a heat exchanger at the base of the oil filter, that is part of the liquid coolant circuit.

There are three types of lubrication condition – 'boundary', 'thin film' and 'hydrodynamic' – and all can exist between the same components, depending on engine speed and load. Boundary lubrication provides a very fine film of oil between the moving parts, not enough to cover those microscopic peaks, and only sufficient for low bearing loads. Thin film lubrication has a thicker layer of oil, the same thickness as the peaks and valleys, so it can cope with higher loads. Hydrodynamic condition has such a thick layer of oil that the metal surfaces don't touch at all, being kept apart by a cushion of oil. Plain bearings, used in big-ends, and sometimes crankshaft main bearings, must have hydrodynamic lubrication. Other types of bearings (ball-bearings or roller-bearings) require a thinner film of oil.

Oil

The oil used in motorcycle engines is far more complicated than the black stuff that comes out of the ground. In fact, synthetic, or part-synthetic oil that is chemically manufactured, is increasingly used in place of mineral oil. Also, a diverse range of additives are used to improve the performance of the oil, including:

Anti-wear agents: Improve oil film strength and so protect components that move against each other.

Anti-foaming agents: Reduce foaming (caused by air mixing with the oil) that would inhibit the oil's ability to lubricate.

Detergents: Enable the oil to hold particles of dirt in suspension, carrying them away to be trapped by the filter.

Corrosion inhibitors: Reduce the rate of oil oxidatition.

Viscosity index improvers: Keep the oil thinner when cold, thicker when hot.

When buying oil, it's important to note which grade and letter code is recommended by the manufacturer for your bike. The two letter code on the back of the oil container is known as the API (American Petroleum Institute) grade. The first letter is 'S' (for spark ignition) and the second denotes the oil's quality – SG, SH and so on. The further along the alphabet, the better the quality, and

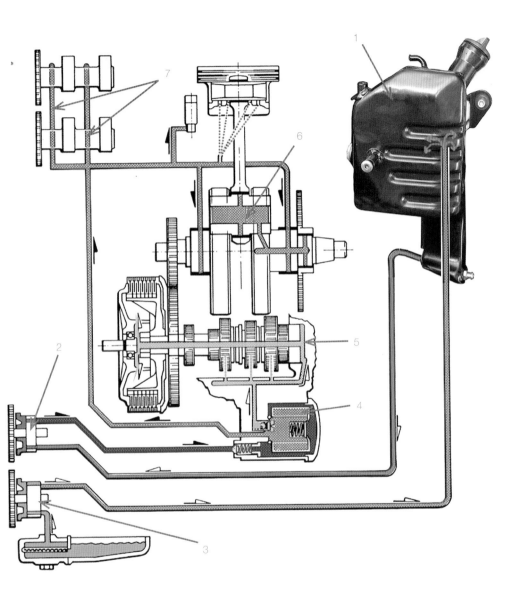

Typical dry sump lubrication circuit for single-cylinder BMW 650: 1 Oil tank, 2 Oil pump (pressure),
3 Oil pump (scavenge), 4 Oil filter, 5 Oil feed to gearbox/clutch, 6 Oil feed to crankshaft,
7 Oil feed to camshafts (BMW)

Triumph Twin with frame-mounted oil cooler (arrowed) positioned to collect maximum airflow. (Veloce)

as better oils are developed, the letters move on towards SZ.

The oil's grade refers to its viscosity or thickness, and is denoted by its SAE grade number. This standard was established by the SAE (Society of Automotive Engineers), and the higher the SAE grade number, the thicker the oil – SAE 10 is relatively thin, SAE 50 relatively thick. The SAE grade is important because oil's viscosity changes with temperature, which has a major effect on the oil's ability to do its job. Oil tends to get thicker when cold, so on a very cold morning oil will take longer to fully protect the bearings. That's why it's best not to start the engine on an open throttle from cold (unless the handbook recommends it): immediate revs from cold cause a lot of wear to oil-starved bearings. Starting with a closed throttle allows the oil time to circulate and warm, while the engine is idling, for those crucial first few seconds.

At the other end of the scale, oil tends to get thinner as temperatures rise. So blasting along a hot Italian autostrada means thinner oil, which has less chance of keeping rubbing surfaces apart.

This is why we have multi-grade oils, which have now been around for over 40 years. The use of viscosity index improvers allows the same oil to suit a wide range of temperatures. So a 10W40 oil operates as a thin SAE10 at freezing temperatures, and a thick SAE40 when the day is hot.

One final point to remember when buying oil: most bikes use the same oil to lubricate the gearbox and clutch, as is used to lubricate the engine. Some car engine oils, however, use friction enhancers that won't be compatible with the clutch – so always make sure you read the small print, or buy a bike-specific oil.

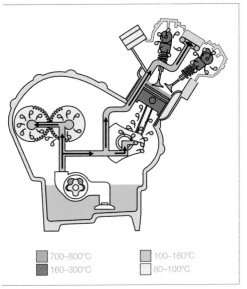

700–800°C   100–160°C
160–300°C   80–100°C

Typical temperature regimes in a four-stroke engine lubrication system. (Castrol Lubricants)

Lubrication systems

There are two main types of lubrication system – wet sump and dry sump. Wet sump is the more common, in which the bottom of the crankcase is used as a reservoir to hold the oil, just like a car. If your bike's oil level is checked with a dipstick or glass window in the crankcase, then you have a wet sump system. In a dry sump, the oil is kept in a separate tank, or sometimes in the tubes of the frame. The advantage, here, is that the engine is lower in height, there's less power loss from oil sloshing, and it delivers a reliable oil supply regardless of extreme lean angles, wheelies, and stoppies. Dry sump is popular with off-road and competition bikes, though it's a more complicated system that needs a second pump (a scavanger pump) to keep the crankcase free of redundant oil.

Both types of system need an oil pump, either the gear or rotor type, to keep the oil circulating. Gear pumps consist of two meshed gears that simply force the oil through as they turn. Rotor pumps have two rotors, one with four lobes, one with five. The four-lobe rotor moves inside the five-lobe, forcing the oil from chamber to chamber and out of the pump. Whatever the type of pump, oil is then fed to wherever it's needed in the engine via a series of galleries, and sometimes external pipes.

Although the pump speed varies with engine speed, the oil pressure it produces can vary according to temperature and the viscosity of the oil. Pressure spikes can potentially damage oil seals and the pump itself, so a pressure-relief valve is fitted that automatically opens above a set pressure, dumping excess oil back into the sump.

The oil filter is a crucial part of the whole system, and often there are two, a coarse filter that prevents larger particles entering the pump, and a finer element filter made of pleated paper that catches microscopic particles. Most bikes now use the car-type spin-on filter that is replaced at every (or every other) oil change.

Two-stroke lubrication

Lubrication is one of the main differences between two- and four-stroke engines. Instead of having a sump of recirculating oil, two-stroke is a 'total loss' system, in which the oil is mixed with the fuel, burnt in the combustion chamber, and exits through the exhaust. It's partly this burnt oil that gives two-strokes (especially older ones) their distinctive smell and blue smoke haze. Two-stroke oil is quite different to that used in a four-stroke engine, and modern synthetic two-stroke oils have reduced the smoke/smell problem significantly, as well as oil consumption.

On older two-strokes, the oil had to be added to the fuel tank in a measured quantity, but modern two-strokes have a separate tank for the oil, plus a pump which delivers the correct amount to be mixed with the fuel downstream of the carburettor, according to throttle opening and speed. Aprilia's DITECH system (Direct Injection Technology) is the most sophisticated of these systems, using electronic injection for the fuel/oil mixture. Unlike a four-stroke engine, this oil cannot be used to lubricate the gearbox and primary drive, which need their own separate oil supply.

Air intake

Air intake systems are more complex than they once were, with the intake being used to suppress noise and boost power, and expected to act in concert with the fuel and exhaust systems.

The most vital part of the air intake, at least for the long-term health of the engine, is the air filter. Even microscopic particles in the atmosphere can cause serious wear inside the engine, and the air filter's job is to stop them getting that far. The most common type of filter is constructed from a sheet of

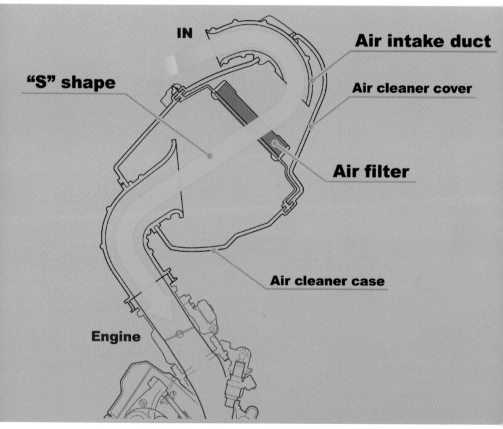

IN

Air intake duct

"S" shape

Air cleaner cover

Air filter

Air cleaner case

Engine

Simple air intake system, showing passage through air filter. (Honda)

A washable sponge air filter is sometimes used on off-road bikes. (Kawasaki)

chemically treated paper containing microscopic pores just large enough to allow air through, but too small to allow microscopic particles to pass. The paper is folded in pleats to maximise surface area. Some off-road bikes and two-strokes use foam impregnated with oil. These must be washed and reoiled regularly. Paper filters are not washable and have to be replaced at regular service intervals – eventually, the pores will block and airflow will be impeded, starving the engine of air and causing an over-rich air/fuel mixture, leading to higher fuel consumption (ie, fewer miles per gallon).

Air box
The air filter is mounted inside the airbox. On modern bikes, especially sports bikes, the plastic airbox is made as large as possible, often using every

The airbox is the engine's 'lung.' (Kawasaki)

Ram air intake system: 1 Air intake, 2 Air box, 3 Air filter. (Kawasaki)

inch of available space between the frame beams, below the fuel tank. Its job is to act as the engine's 'lung,' with a reservoir of clean, relatively calm air, that can be drawn from as needed. The calmer the air, the more even its pressure, which is good news, as fluctuating air pressure will upset the fuelling system. Another airbox job is to suppress intake noise. When thinking of noise, most of us think about what comes out of the exhaust pipes, but intake noise can be a significant contributor. The airbox has to be carefully designed to dampen noise without impeding the airflow.

Sports bikes often have air intakes at the very front of the fairing, to draw cool air that hasn't been warmed by coming past the radiator. Cooler air is denser and carries more oxygen, and this means a bigger burn in the combustion chamber when added to the right quantity of fuel. These intakes also offer the prospect of making use of the bike's forward motion to ram air into the airbox as fast as possible. It sounds like a sort of free supercharging for a bike travelling at high speeds, but in practice, the actual power boost is marginal – only around 1 per cent at 100mph. Still, they do look cool.

Complete intake (in blue) and exhaust (in red) system. (Kawasaki)

The fuel system

Motorcycle engines run on a mixture of air and fuel, and for many decades this was supplied by relatively crude carburettors. Increasing standards of performance and rideability, plus emissions legislation, have forced manufacturers to adopt electronic fuel-injection on most bikes, that is part of a complete engine management system.

The fuel system's job is to bring fuel and air together, and deliver them to the combustion chamber at the right time, in the right amount. The key to this is extremely accurate metering of fuel over widely differing conditions and engine loads, plus maintaining the optimum air/fuel ratio.

Some people assume that the more fuel that goes into the air/fuel mixture, the more power you get. But the engine needs oxygen as well as fuel to make an efficient combustion, and greatly increasing the proportion of fuel in the mix will result in very poor running. In fact, there is an optimum air/fuel ratio of about 14.7:1. This is known as the stoichiometric ratio, at which all the oxygen combines with all the fuel, and everything burns during combustion, with no unburnt leftovers. The exception is cold starting, when the ratio needs to be artificially rich, as fuel in a cold engine has difficulty vapourising. The job of the modern fuel system is to supply something as close to the ideal air/fuel mix as possible, with tweaks to the stoichiometric ratio where needed.

The basic fuel system consists of a tank that delivers fuel to the carburettor or injection system by gravity, or under pressure by a pump. A fuel filter between the tank and the rest of the system prevents impurities entering the system. There may be a manual fuel tap, to cut off the supply when the bike is parked, but this is increasingly being superseded by an automatic vacuum tap, which opens when the engine is started and closes when the engine is switched off.

Electric fuel pump housed within tank (cutaway here). (Kawasaki)

Carburettor

The carburettor's dominance in motorcycle fuel systems has really been overtaken by fuel-injection, but it remains in use on smaller, cheaper machines, and some off-road bikes. The basic carburettor consists of a smooth-sided tube, which narrows in the middle before widening again. This narrowing, called a venturi, has the effect of speeding airflow through the tube, lowering its pressure at the venturi. Below the venturi is a small reservoir of fuel (the float chamber), which is kept at a constant level by a float and needle valve. A narrow tube, the main jet, rises from the float chamber and pokes through into the venturi. The lower air pressure in the venturi draws fuel from

the float chamber up the main jet and into the venturi, where it mixes with the airflow as tiny droplets. The more even the mix, the better the combustion.

The rider controls the air/fuel mixture by means of a throttle. At very low throttle openings, or when the engine is idling, there isn't a low enough pressure in the venturi to draw the fuel through, so a bypass circuit, the pilot jet, is provided to trickle in the very small amounts of fuel needed, independently of the throttle.

For more power, the rider's control of the twistgrip takes over, and this is where we differentiate between the two main types of carburettor – slide and constant velocity (CV). The throttle inside of a slide carburettor consists of a slide that moves up as the twistgrip turns, opening the carburettor venturi, and allowing more air/fuel mixture to pass. However, the increased airflow on its own isn't enough to draw sufficient fuel up from the float chamber, so a tapered needle is fitted to the bottom of the slide that fits neatly into the main jet. At low throttle, this needle nearly blocks the jet, allowing only a small amount of fuel through. As the throttle is opened, the needle rises, increasing the size of the opening and allowing extra fuel through.

However, the slide carburettor does have a fundamental flaw. If the throttle is snapped open from idle or low revs, a large volume of extra air is drawn into the carburettor. But as the engine speed is still low, the air is moving slowly, not fast enough to draw the increased amount of fuel from the jet. The air/fuel mixture that arrives in the combustion chamber is too lean, causing hesitation and even stalling. Pre-injection sports bikes get around this problem with an accelerator pump, which delivers extra fuel when the throttle is opened suddenly.

The CV carburettor also gets around this problem, and works so well that it has become the dominant type. These carburettors still use a slide, but instead of the slide being directly controlled from the twistgrip, it rises or falls according to the difference in air pressure between the inlet manifold and the outside air – the twistgrip simply controls a butterfly throttle, immediately downstream of the slide. The top of the carburettor is divided in two by an airtight diaphragm – air above the diaphragm varies with engine load, and the air below it is kept at atmospheric pressure. Opening the butterfly throttle causes a reduction in air pressure above the diaphragm, which lifts, causing the slide and tapered needle to rise, allowing more fuel through. However sharply the butterfly is snapped open, the diaphragm will only lift the slide when the air pressure is sufficiently reduced, so a sudden surplus of air, and a lean mixture, is avoided.

Fuel-injection
Instead of relying on differences in air pressure to draw fuel into the inlet manifold, fuel-injection injects it at very high pressure. Although thought of as new technology, fuel-injection was in quite widespread use in aircraft during the 1940s, and the first production motorcycle to use electronic fuel-injection was the Kawasaki Z1000-H1 in 1980.

The increasing sophistication and falling price of electronics has made injection systems much more effective and affordable. They are now able to deliver a precise amount of fuel extremely accurately, depending on a wide range of constantly monitored parameters. The typical system consists not just of the injectors and the high pressure pump that supplies them, but sensors that measure airflow into the engine, the engine speed, crankshaft angle, air temperature and density, engine temperature, and throttle position. The throttle, incidentally, is a simple butterfly valve, the same as in the CV carburettor, and is housed in a throttle body (one for each cylinder) just upstream of the inlet valve.

The information collected by these sensors is sent to an electronic control unit (ECU). This contains a multi-dimensional 'map' that tells the engine how much fuel (and when) to inject for each given set of conditions – load, engine speed, air temperature, and so on. The ECU then calculates how long the injector needs to open for, and sends that information to the injector in the form of a precise electrical pulse. The pulse opens the injector, and the correct amount of fuel, at high pressure, is sprayed into the throttle body, where it mixes with the air and is delivered to the combustion chamber. All of this happens extremely quickly – the typical injector opening time is 1.5 to 10 milliseconds.

1 Injector, 2 High pressure fuel rail, 3 Butterfly valves. (Kawasaki)

The injector itself consists of a valve body and needle valve. When the ECU sends it an electrical command, a solenoid coil inside the injector lifts the valve from its seat, allowing the high pressure fuel through. The fuel is kept at high pressure by a pump – switch on the ignition on a fuel-injected engine, and you'll often hear a buzzing that last just a few seconds. That's the fuel pump pressurising the delivery system.

There are different types of injection systems, but motorcycles tend use the same types – indirect injection (fuel is injected into the throttle body, rather than directly into the combustion chamber), and sequential injection, in which each injector (there are sometimes two per cylinder) injects just before the inlet valve for its cylinder opens. On car injection systems, injectors may fire all at the same time, or in pairs. The sequential type gives the most precise fuelling.

The injection system still may not give perfect fuelling all of the time, and to check this, a sensor in the exhaust checks on the amount of oxygen coming out of the cylinder. If the oxygen level incorrect, it sends a message to the ECU, which adjusts the fuelling accordingly, a form of self-correction unavailable to the humble carburettor. However, all this sophistication comes at a price, which is why carburettors are still used on most scooters and small commuter motorcycles.

Ignition system

For the air/fuel mixture of a petrol engine to burn, it needs a spark to ignite it, and that's the job of the ignition system. This consists of a low tension (voltage) electrical current (usually from the battery) boosted to high tension by a coil. This pulse of high tension

(HT) current is supplied to a sparkplug, where it jumps across an air gap, igniting the air/fuel mixture. All of this happens very quickly: at 6000rpm (only medium revs for many bike engines), the ignition system must supply 50 sparks per second to each sparkplug.

Sparkplug
The sparkplug screws into the combustion chamber, where it has to endure high pressures, vibration, and gas temperatures of up to 2500 degrees C. It consists of an electrode that carries the HT pulse, and is surrounded by a ceramic insulator that protects it from heat and prevents electrical leakage. The lower half is contained by a threaded metal case that allows the plug to be screwed into the cylinder head. This also contains the earth electrode – for the electrical circuit to be completed, the HT spark must go to earth (ground) after it has jumped the air gap.

Although the plug has to be protected from excessive heat, it does work best at 400-800 degrees C. Below that temperature, deposits will form on the electrodes, eventually interfering with the spark and causing misfiring. At higher temperatures, the heat of the plug itself can cause the air/fuel mixture to ignite prematurely. This is called pre-ignition (also referred to as knocking, pinging or pinking), and it's bad for any engine, increasing the temperature and pressure in the cylinder while the piston is still on its upward stroke. Pre-ignition can seriously damage the engine if allowed to go unchecked.

Ignition timing
The problem of pre-ignition neatly highlights another vital job of the ignition system – producing a spark at precisely the right moment. Ideally, this is a very short time before TDC (top dead centre, or the point when the piston is at the

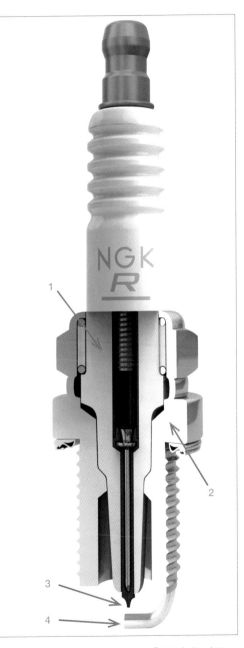

Anatomy of a sparkplug: 1 Ceramic insulator, 2 Metal case, 3 Electrode, 4 Earth electrode. (NGK)

very top of its stroke). When the air/fuel mixture ignites, it doesn't explode, but burns, the flame front racing across the combustion chamber at up to 50 metres per second. The faster the engine is running, the earlier the spark has to occur to give sufficient time for ignition to take place, so every ignition system has provision for making the spark occur earlier (advancing the ignition) as engine revs rise.

On older bikes, ignition systems were mechanical, but most current ignition systems (except on simple carburettor bikes) are an integrated part of the engine management system, working in concert with the fuel-injection, if fitted. As with the injectors, sensors on various parts of the engine send information to the ECU on engine speed, throttle position, crankshaft position, etc. The ECU holds a 'map,' which tells it exactly when to fire the spark according to the particular mix of engine conditions at any one time. The result is a more accurate spark and a cleaner-running engine.

Exhaust & pollution control

On the face of it, the exhaust system looks like a very simple component – one or more pipes and a silencer (muffler), to take exhaust gases away from the engine, quietening them in the process. In practice, it's a lot more complex than that, which is why bolt-on aftermarket systems rarely produce extra power (though they may well deliver on noise).

The exhaust pipe exits the engine at the exhaust port, and usually runs down the front of the engine and underneath it. Often referred to as a downpipe, there is usually one per cylinder (large displacement single- and twin-cylinder bikes may have two), all of them

Cutaway exhaust silencer, often mounted under the seat on a sports bike. (Kawasaki)

Downpipes serving a four-cylinder engine, one pipe per cylinder. (Yamaha)

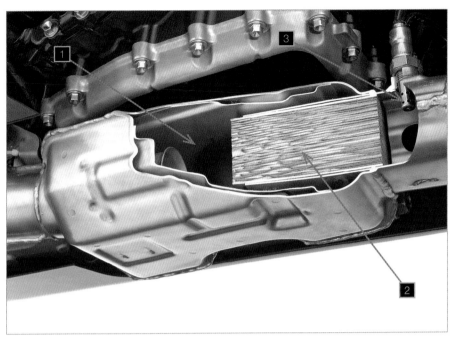

Cutaway of an exhaust collector box: 1 Pre-chamber, 2 Catalyst, 3 Lambda sensor. (Kawasaki)

meeting in a collector box underneath the engine/gearbox. The pipes may be painted or chromed, and are increasingly of stainless steel to combat corrosion. The collector box will lead to one or two silencers.

This is where it gets more complicated: the silencer has to quieten the sound of combustion (which would otherwise be deafening), but do so in a way which restricts the flow of exhaust gases as little as possible. Incidentally, we've used the English term 'silencer' here, but the American 'muffler' is a more accurate description of what it actually does.

The noise is muffled either by reflection or absorption. Most modern road bikes have a reflection system, which slows the rushing gases a little as they expand into the silencer, then absorbs more energy by making them pass through perforated baffles, or a tortuous path of direction changes. This breaks the big sound waves into smaller ones, some of which cancel each other out.

The baffles may be supplemented by sound absorbent material, which on a smaller number of bikes is used as the main agent, usually rock wool or basalt wool (the same material used for loft insulation), which makes for a lighter, simpler silencer.

Pressure waves

Absorbing sound isn't the exhaust system's only job. It can actually aid cylinder scavenging and power output by exploiting the pressure waves of gases which travel through the system. It does this by bouncing some of the pressure wave back through the pipe towards the engine, preventing the

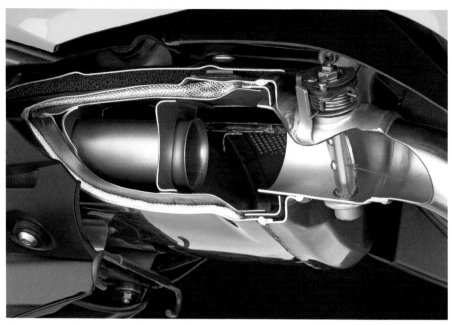

Cutaway of underseat exhaust silencer. Butterfly valve (arrowed) creates back pressure. (Kawasaki)

Expansion chamber in a two-stroke exhaust improves efficiency. (Kawasaki)

next air/fuel mixture load from escaping straight into the exhaust. This is particularly important for two strokes, so, often, an expansion chamber is used to create reverse pulses. When the exhaust valve closes, the pressure wave is bounced off down the pipe again, creating negative pressure at the exhaust port, ready to suck out the next wave of exhaust gas.

By careful design of the length of each pipe, the exhaust can use these pressure waves to best advantage. It's much more critical on a two-stroke engine than a four-stroke, and was pioneered on East German MZ racers in the 1950s. The exhaust can only really be tuned to take advantage of pressure waves within a certain rev band, and the result is always a compromise, though some four-stroke exhausts have valves which vary the aperture of the exhaust according to engine speed, and thus increase the width of the band.

Pollution control
Almost all exhaust systems on fuel-injected bikes now incorporate a catalytic convertor. These have become necessary as concern over air pollution has grown, and legislation has become tighter. The catalyst, or 'cat,' is a dense honeycomb of metal, its internal

Catalyst (arrowed) in this cutaway exhaust system is a honeycomb of rare metals. (Kawasaki)

surfaces coated with rare metals such as platinum, palladium and rhodium. These are the catalysts, and as the exhaust gases pass through, they are converted by chemical reaction. Harmful hydrocarbons, carbon monoxide and oxides of nitrogen (HC, CO and Nox, respectively) become more benign water vapour, carbon dioxide and oxygen. More than 90 per cent of the noxious gases are converted, so the cat does a good job. It works best running hot, at 280 to 750 degrees C, and placing it within the exhaust helps it to heat up quickly.

The cat is not a magic box that works on its own; to be effective, it has to be combined with the overall engine design. Since incomplete combustion is the source of pollution, much work has been done in recent years to improve the burn inside the combustion chamber, reducing pollution at source through engine management, fuel-injection and component design.

The catalyst is part of this whole system, but it can only work well if the air/fuel ratio is very close to stoichiometric (see page 13). To ensure that it is, a sensor – the lambda sensor – is sited in the exhaust port and keeps the engine management system informed of how much oxygen is contained in the exhaust gas. The ECU can then calculate what the air/fuel ratio is and whether it needs adjusting to keep the cat working efficiently.

Lambda sensor measures the amount of oxygen in the exhaust gases. (Bosch)

three
Transmission

A motorcycle transmission connects the engine to the rear wheel, and although details may differ, the job it has to do is the same. Most bikes' transmissions consist of a primary drive direct from engine to clutch, a manual gearbox, and final drive to the wheel by chain, toothed belt, or shaft. The transmission's job is two-fold: to disconnect the engine from the rear wheel when the bike is stopped (the clutch) and to provide gearing to boost the engine's effective torque.

The petrol engine is not as torquey as we like to think it is. A steam engine or electric motor produces high torque from virtually zero revs, but the petrol unit is puny by comparison. Even a big Harley-Davidson V-twin only produces its prodigious torque over a relatively limited range of engine speeds.

How gears work

The solution to an engine's limited torque range is gearing, for which cycling is a good analogy. Human legs, like the petrol engine, work best over a limited range of speeds. Take a 24-speed mountain bike and try to set off in top gear, or stay in that gear uphill: it's very hard work. Try to get your motorcycle moving in top gear, and the engine also has a tough job, but change down to a low gear and it becomes easy.

Gears work by changing the speed differential between the power source (your legs, or your bike's engine) and the rear wheel. If the drive gear and the gear being driven are the same size, with the same number of teeth, then their speeds will be the same.

But if the driven gear is twice as big, with, for example, 30 teeth, it will run at half the speed. In other words, the rear wheel will be running at half the speed for a given engine speed (say 30mph at 4000rpm), where the engine is producing a decent amount of torque (instead of at 2000rpm, where the engine isn't producing so much).

The difference in gear size is known as the gear ratio. For the example just given, it would be 2:1 – though handbooks often refer to the number of teeth as well, which in this case would be 15/30T. That's a very simple example of 'gearing down' (reducing the gear ratio to increase torque), and in practice, every part of the transmission apart from the clutch – that is, primary drive, gearbox, final drive – alter the gear ratio between engine and rear wheel, through the use of different-sized gears or sprockets. Even with all that help, the gearbox will still need to offer a wide choice of different ratios, usually six.

Primary drive

The primary drive is the first stage in transferring the engine's torque from the crankshaft to the rear wheel. Its job is to transmit crankshaft movement to the clutch, and on modern bikes this is normally done through two large gears that mesh together. As well as being efficient, gear drives are very strong and, if kept well lubricated, don't need maintenance. They're also well suited to high-revving engines, being unaffected by centrifugal forces, so they are ideal for modern motorcycles.

Although gear drives are now very common, chain primary drive was once the standard method. These were quiet (and efficient when properly adjusted), but needed adjusting periodically, unless an automatic chain tensioner was fitted, and their life span was shorter than that of gears.

One final word on gear drives, and something that chain drive doesn't suffer from: with just two gears involved, the output shaft will rotate in the opposite direction to the input shaft, so it has to be reversed again further along the system if we aren't to end up with six reverse gears. Fortunately, the direction of rotation changes a number of times through several sets of gears, so if the engineers have done their sums correctly, all should be well by the time the rotation reaches the rear wheel.

Manual clutch

The job of the clutch is to disconnect the engine from the rest of the transmission, allowing the bike to be stationary with the engine running, and to change gear ratio in a manual gearbox. In the pioneer days of motorcycling, bikes did without a clutch, using direct drive (by belt) between engine and rear wheel. This worked well enough over a low speed range, but involved stopping the engine whenever the bike was brought to a halt, then push starting – a clutch is a lot more convenient.

A simple clutch has two plates, one on the engine side, one on the gearbox side, and when these are touching the friction between them transmits drive. When they are pulled apart (via the handlebar clutch lever), the drive is lost and the engine is disconnected. Movable plates allow for a gradual take-up of drive, essential for smooth getaways.

On bikes with transverse crankshafts (that is most bikes, apart from BMW flat-twins and Moto Guzzi V-twins) the clutch is multi-plate, with several pairs of plates. This keeps the clutch compact; a large diameter single-plate clutch would be very awkward to accommodate. The multi-plate clutch consists of three main parts: the plates, the housing (sometimes called the basket), and the centre. The clutch housing is mounted on the gearbox input shaft, but is free

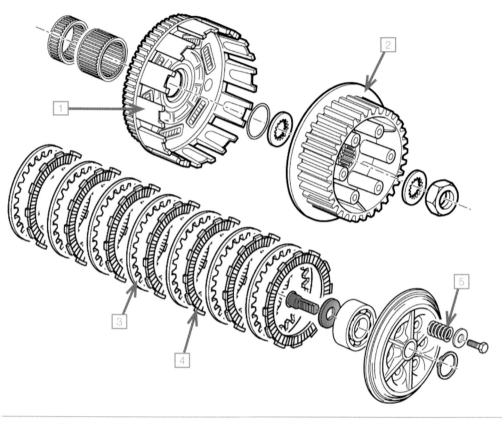

Wet multi-plate clutch: 1 Clutch housing (or basket), 2 Clutch centre, 3 Plain plate (x7 in this example), 4 Friction plate (x7 in this example), 5 Clutch spring. (BMW)

to turn independently of the shaft. It's in direct drive with the crankshaft, so while the engine is turning, the housing is also turning. The clutch centre, on the other hand, which fits inside the housing, is bolted to the gearbox input shaft – when it turns, the input shaft turns.

The clutch plates fit in the gap between the centre and housing. There are two types of plates, layered alternately: friction plates, that have external tabs that slot into the housing; and plain plates, that have inner tabs that locate with the clutch centre. The plates are held in contact with each other by an outer pressure plate and springs.

With the clutch lever out, the plates stay in contact, making the clutch housing and centre turn as a single unit, transmitting drive from engine to gearbox. When the lever is pulled in, they are pulled very slightly apart, breaking the link between clutch housing and centre. Now the housing can keep turning with the engine, but the centre can spin to a stop.

Slipper clutch (mechanism arrowed) reduces conflict between engine and braking torque. (Yamaha)

The capacity of the clutch to transmit drive can be altered by changing the size or number of plates. They invariably run in oil (which sounds a bit odd for a component that depends on friction to do its job), but more and/ or larger plates can make up for this, and the friction material is designed to run in oil. Some clutches on high end sports bikes or racers are run dry, which saves weight. They may also have a slipper clutch, which allows downward changes without using the clutch lever. This isn't for convenience: sudden manual downshifts (or braking) can cause the rear wheel to hop up and down when the braking torque exerted by the engine exceeds that of the transmission. The slipper clutch, either mechanically or pneumatically, slips the clutch momentarily, which ameliorates this effect.

Another variation is the single-plate dry clutch used on, for example, BMW flat-twins. These bikes can use this car-type clutch because the crankshaft is mounted longitudinally, so the clutch can be mounted on the end, as in a car – with fewer space issues, one large plate can be used.

Automatic clutch

Until recently, automatic clutches, which do away with the need for a manual clutch lever, have been restricted to scooters and mopeds. These have often used a mechanism that engages the clutch by centrifugal force, acting on weights or balls as engine speed increases.

More recently, more sophisticated automatic clutches have begun to appear on large motorcycles. Honda's dual clutch transmission (see page 49) is a prominent example, but the first in recent times was the electronic clutch fitted to Yamaha's FJR1300AS. In this case, the clutch is controlled by the ECU, which adjusts ignition timing, too, to give smooth gear changes in around 0.2 seconds. Gears are still shifted manually, either by a conventional foot lever or by pushbuttons, making this a semi-automatic system. With the increased popularity of semi-automatic transmission on high-performance cars, it looks likely that its use will increase among motorcycles.

Semi-automatic pushbutton gear changes are offered on increasing numbers of bikes. (Yamaha)

Manual gearbox

Internally, a gearbox looks more complicated than it actually is, a mechanically operated device that allows the rider to shift between the various gear ratios. Each ratio has a pair of gears, so a six-speed gearbox will contain twelve gears. The gearbox has two shafts, and one gear from each pair is mounted on the input shaft (sometimes called the mainshaft), the other on the output shaft (also known as the countershaft or layshaft).

Each pair of gears is in constant mesh, that is, in direct contact all the time, whether or not their ratio is the one selected. So changing gear does not involve forcing gears into mesh with each other, which would be a quick means of losing all the teeth!

If the ratio is not selected, one of these gears will be locked to its shaft and spinning with it, while the other 'freewheels' on its shaft, thus not transmitting drive. In order to transmit drive, the gear next to it (which is locked to its shaft and therefore turning) is slid along splines on the shaft until it touches the freewheeling gear. 'Dogs' or protrusions from the locked gear engage with equivalent holes in the freewheeling gear, locking it into engagement and transmitting drive.

It's worth noting here that a motorcycle gearbox, unlike the car equivalent, does not have syncromesh. Syncromesh synchronises the speed of the gearwheel being selected with that of the shaft it is mounted on. The dog system used in a motorcycle gearbox is simpler, lighter, and takes up less space, but it does require you to blip the throttle as you change down, to equalise (or nearly so) the speeds of the various spinning components.

Sliding the gears along the shaft

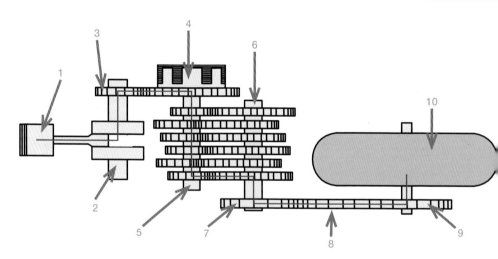

A typical transmission layout, viewed from above, illustrates the path power transmission – red line – takes between piston and rear wheel (it could also travel via any one of the other five gear sets). 1 Piston, 2 Crankshaft, 3 Primary drive gear 4 Clutch, 5 Mainshaft, 6 Layshaft (Countrershaft), 7 Gearbox sprocket, 8 Drive chain, 9 Final drive sprocket, 10 Rear wheel. (Castrol Lubricants)

is the job of the selector mechanism. When the gearshift lever is moved, this turns a selector drum that, in turn, moves one of three selector forks. The fork pushes on the gear, sliding it along the shaft. Slots or tracks cut into the drum move the fork in the right direction to select the next gear. The drum has a system of limiters that ensure that for each full movement of the gearlever, the selector fork will move just far enough to select the next gear. At the same time, another of the forks will move to shift the previous gear out of engagement.

Dual clutch transmission
Made by Honda, the dual clutch transmission (DCT) is a semi-automatic system that seeks to give the best of both worlds – the convenience of an automatic clutch with the choice of automatic or manual gear selection. Launched on the VFR1200, a simplified version is now offered on the NC700 commuter/all-rounder, and is likely to be

used on other Hondas in the future.

DCT is a six-speed transmission, using pairs of gears and selector forks, just like a conventional manual gearbox. But instead of a single manual clutch, the Honda transmission has two, one controlling gears 1, 3 and 5 (plus starting from rest), the other controlling gears 2, 4 and 6. The clutches are operated hydraulically, working in sync with the selectors to effect smooth gear

Honda dual clutch transmission gives automatic clutch operation. (Honda)

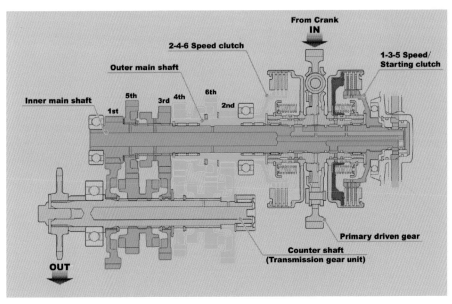

Cross section of Honda DCT showing six-speed gearbox. (Honda)

changes. They are masterminded by the bike's ECU, meaning that fuelling and ignition adjustments can be combined with gear changes.

The DCT rider can select auto mode, in which case the ECU will decide when to change up or down between the gears. There's the choice of normal or sport mode, too: in sport mode, DCT will change gear at higher revs. If the rider can't resist changing gear him or herself, selecting manual mode allows changing gear via paddle shifters. Either way, there's no clutch lever.

Full automatics

Fully automatic transmissions are restricted to scooters, where convenience and ease of riding are the top priorities. Known as Constantly Variable Transmissions (CVT), they are extremely simple, giving an infinite number of ratios between upper and lower limits. The CVT uses a V-belt connecting two V-shaped pulleys, one on the end of the crankshaft, the other at the final drive. Because a CVT only works effectively with a short distance between the two pulleys, the engine must either be mounted close to the rear wheel (as on a scooter), or an additional drive must be added. On larger scooters, such as the Yamaha T-Max, an additional chain drive transmits from the rear pulley to the rear wheel.

The pulleys are split into two, one half fixed in place, the other free to slide on a shaft, thus changing the effective diameter of the pulley. Just as with different sized gear wheels, changing the size of each pulley relative to the other changes the gear ratio between them. As the sliding pulley-half moves out from the fixed half, the belt moves down, and the pulley diameter gets smaller. When it slides

in, the belt is forced upwards as the diameter increases. All of this is done automatically, according to conditions, by means of a simple centrifugal mechanism on the drive (front) pulley, which moves the sliding half inwards as engine speed increases. The driven (rear) pulley has a spring that responds in the opposite direction. In theory, the transmission should always be in the correct ratio, whether accelerating, cruising, riding up hill or down.

Another type of automatic transmission (though so far only used on Honda's DN-01) is the Human-Friendly Transmission (HFT), an attempt by Honda to make a fully automatic transmission suitable for a motorcycle. It is hydraulic in operation, using the angle between two swash plates to change the gear ratio. Unlike the DCT, there is no semi-automatic option.

Final drive

The final drive, as its name suggests, is the last stage in the torque's journey from engine to rear wheel. It can be a roller chain, a car-type shaft, or a toothed belt, and they all incorporate a final gear ratio reduction, typically between 2.5:1 and 3:1.

Chain drive

Chain drive is overwhelmingly dominant, and has been since the 1920s. It has several advantages, being relatively light, affordable and compact. It's also the most efficient final drive, at least when the chain is well lubed and adjusted.

Its downside is that the chain needs a lot of maintenance. Exposed to road dirt, grit, and water, it will wear rapidly if not regularly cleaned and lubricated. Also, chains stretch with

Chain drive is efficient when well maintained. (Yamaha)

use as each of the many moving joints wear, so they have to be adjusted to the correct freeplay on a regular basis. The sprockets on which the chain runs (one on the gearbox output shaft, one bolted to the rear wheel) also wear relatively quickly. Some riders fit automatic chain oilers, to keep the chain lubed and reduce maintenance.

One innovation has been the O-ring or X-ring chain. This plugs the space between the side plates of the chain with a seal, allowing every roller bush to have its lubricant sealed in at the manufacturing stage. O- and X-ring

Chain O-rings are situated between the sideplates.

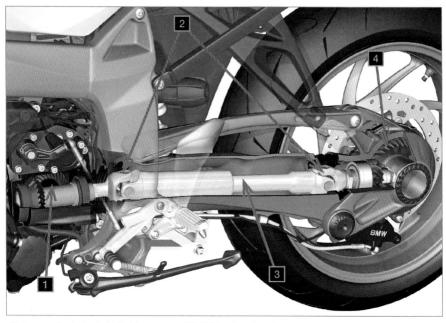

Cutaway of a typical shaft drive system (BMW Paralever): 1 Bevel drive from gearbox output shaft, 2 Universal joints, 3 Driveshaft, 4 Final drive bevel gears. (BMW)

chains still need lubricating, to keep the seals pliable. Heavier and more expensive than a standard roller chain, they do have a much longer service life, and are standard on most medium and big bikes with chain drive.

Chains were once joined by a split link (still used on the small commuter machines), but are now usually joined by a 'soft link' or riveted chain, which has a master link from which the rivets can be removed using a special tool. Endless chains, with no join at all, are the strongest, and are used on some high-performance bikes.

Chain sizes are listed as three digits – 520, 525, 530, and so on. Surprisingly, these are based on imperial measurements. The first letter refers to the chain's pitch (the distance between two pins) in eighths of an inch – '5' is ⅝ inch, '6' is ⁶⁄₈ inch, and so on.

The second and third letters denote the width of the rollers in eightieths of an inch – '20' is $^{20}\!/_{80}$ inch. The third number is sometimes changed to denote a stronger version of the chain with thicker side plates.

Shaft drive
Shaft drive has become the standard for big touring machines, which makes a lot of sense. Apart from a need to change the oil in the rear bevel casing, it's maintenance free, and for this reason alone is better suited to long distance riding (especially in poor conditions) than chain drive. All the moving parts are sealed, protecting them from wear, and making the whole rear end of the bike cleaner. The universal joints will need replacing eventually, but often a shaft drive will outlive the engine that powers it.

Of course, there are downsides. Shaft drive is expensive and heavy, amounting to a great deal of unsprung weight (weight that moves with the suspension, but isn't supported by it). It's also relatively inefficient compared to a chain in good condition. These problems are less significant in an expensive, heavy, powerful touring bike. Earlier shaft drive systems were prone to making the rear of the bike rise up under acceleration, an effect of the torque of the fast turning shaft, but modern systems have all but eliminated this.

On bikes with longitudinal crankshafts, shaft drive is easy to fit, following the same pattern as a car. But with the more common transverse crankshaft, an extra pair of bevel gears needs to added to turn the drive through 90 degrees from the end of the crankshaft. The shaft drive has to be flexible, to move up and down with the rear suspension, so one or two universal or constant velocity joints are added at either end of the shaft.

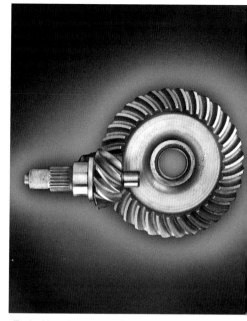

Typical bevel gears used to turn power path through 90 degrees. (BMW)

Toothed belt drive

The earliest motorcycles used belt drive, albeit smooth V-belts that slipped badly in the wet. Modern toothed belt drives are quite different, the teeth engaging with toothed pulleys to prevent slip. Modern belt drive was pioneered by Harley Davidson in 1980 and is now fitted across its range, as well as some other cruisers and BMW's mid-size F800S and ST.

The belt is made of a polyurethane compound, reinforced by kevlar cords running longitudinally, and it has several advantages over a chain drive. The belt does not need adjusting in most cases, nor lubrication. They are slightly bulkier than a chain and do need changing at a specified interval (30-60,000 miles), but, otherwise, are maintenance-free. They are also quieter than a chain and provide a smoother drive.

Toothed belt drive has several advantages over chain drive. (BMW)

four

Cycle parts

Sometimes referred to as the rolling chassis, the frame, suspension, wheels, tyres, and brakes are quite literally the 'cycle' parts of a motorcyle. Important though the engine is to how a bike goes and to its character, the cycle parts are also fundamental to how the bike performs. All of these components are based around a series of compromises, designed to best suit the type of bike and what is expected of it.

BMW K1300 chassis: beam frame, Telelever front suspension, Paralever rear. (BMW)

The frame

The frame is a motorcycle's skeleton – it holds everything together and gives the whole a structural integrity. All major components – engine, transmission and suspension – are attached to the frame, which has several different jobs to do.

Frame geometry

As well as providing a location for all the important bits, the frame has to provide suitable geometry, wheelbase and centre of gravity. It must keep the wheels in line, even under the incredible stresses of hard cornering, braking and acceleration. And it has to keep the steering head in a vertical plane, and the swingarm in a horizontal plane, as the rider is zipping along his/her favourite twisty road.

There are a few measurements that make up a frame's geometry and,

fundamentally, each measurement is a compromise: they all affect each other, and their values will depend on what sort of bike the frame is destined for.

Taken together, these dimensions will determine the bike's weight distribution, which in turn determines where its centre of gravity is. A high centre of gravity increases weight transfer under acceleration (to the rear) or braking (to the front), meaning better grip. That's obviously a good thing, as more rear tyre grip under acceleration reduces the chance of wheelspin, and more front tyre grip under braking reduces the risk of locking up. Under cornering, a high centre of gravity also needs less of a lean angle for a given radius (sharpness) of corner. On the other hand, a low centre of gravity makes a bike more responsive to steering input, easier to control at low speed, and feel less top heavy.

Simple aluminium frame and subframe for single-cylinder off-road bike. (BMW)

Now for the dimensions. The wheelbase – the distance between the two wheel centres – is the most obvious to the casual observer. In general, the longer the wheelbase, the more stable a bike is in a straight line, and the less responsive when cornering – that's why a Harley-Davidson ElectraGlide has a long wheelbase, and a Yamaha R6 a short one. A long wheelbase also reduces weight transfer, making wheelspin and wheel locking more likely – but for the extra stability and room a long wheelbase gives, this is a reasonable trade-off for a tourer or cruiser bike. Conversely, a shorter wheelbase gives a 'twitchier,' more responsive ride: just right for a focused sports bike.

Trail, another aspect of frame geometry, is the distance at ground level between a vertical line drawn through the front wheel axis, and another drawn through the steering axis. It's affected by the diameter of the wheels, angle of the steering tube, and offset of the fork triple clamp (ie, how far the forks are mounted in front of the steering tube). Closely related to trail is rake, the angle of the steering tube, measured in degrees.

Rake and trail, along with wheelbase, are fundamental to how a bike will steer. A relatively steep steering angle (say 24 degrees) and short trail

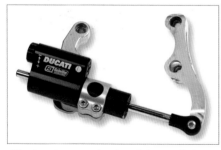

Steering damper calms handlebar oscillations.
(Ducati)

will give quicker, more responsive steering than a shallower steering angle (say 32 degrees) and longer trail. We all like responsive steering, but the downside is that the bike can seem twitchy and nervous: this suits sports bike riders, but is anathema to someone who wants a stable, hassle-free ride.

Frame types & materials

Although all frames must do the same set of tasks, they come in different forms. Some use the engine itself as part of the frame – the engine forms the lower part and acts as what is called a stressed member. This makes the frame smaller, simpler and lighter, but the engine needs to be stronger than it would otherwise be.

From the early pioneer days, motorcycles have used tubular steel frames. Steel, regarded by many as yesterday's material, has many advantages as a frame material. It's strong, easily shaped and welded (and repaired, when things go wrong), as well as being low cost, which is all good news for bike manufacturers.

The traditional cradle frame (so-called because the engine and gearbox are 'cradled' by a network of tubes) is welded together, and works very well. There's usually a single top tube, and one or two down tubes running from the steering head, below the engine, and up to the swingarm pivot. Tubular steel cradle frames are still used on many new bikes, thanks to their strength and low cost. Their biggest drawback is weight.

The trellis frame is a variation, again made of steel tubes (either round- or square-section) welded together. These are all short, straight tubes, welded into a series of triangulations for maximum strength. With the engine bolted underneath as a stressed member, this makes for an extremely rigid and strong

Tubular steel frames are still favoured for their relatively low cost.

structure, though it's more expensive to make than a cradle frame. Ducati is the best known user, though others have followed suit.

Another variation is the spine frame, using a single spine (either a wide diameter tube or pressed steel) from which all the components are hung. It has often been used on scooters, and the first generation of modern Triumphs used a spine frames.

So, steel has its advantages but, as sports bikes became ever more focussed in the 1980s, aluminium alloy made its first appearance in mainstream production. Aluminium alloy is only one-third the weight of steel, and one-third the strength – but that doesn't mean you have to use three times as much, as it's also stiffer. Along with aluminium alloy came the beam, or perimeter frame, consisting of two massive box-section beams into which the engine is bolted, with a rear subframe to support

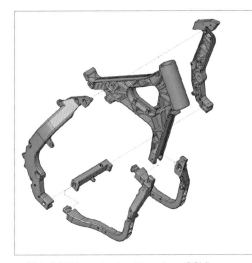

This CCM frame is glued together. (CCM)

the seat and other parts. All beam frames use the engine as a stressed member, and they are particularly light and strong. Some have actually been made of steel box-sections. The beam frame has become very widespread and the frame of choice for most sports and sports touring bikes.

Suspension

Motorcycle suspension has to absorb undulations in the road and keep the wheels in contact with the ground, to give acceptable comfort and handling. Without suspension, the bike would be almost impossible to control. Although various types of suspension have been tried, including rubber blocks, the combination of steel coil springs plus fluid (sometimes gas) for damping, has become the overwhelmingly dominant form. Damping is needed because coil springs, after absorbing a bump, have a tendency to continue oscillating up and down, in ever smaller movements. Damping literally dampens this down, returning the spring to its neutral state as soon as possible.

The concept of 'unsprung weight' is important to the working of suspension, as the less of it there is, the better the suspension works. Sprung weight is everything that the suspension supports – engine, frame, fuel tank and so on. When you sit on your bike, everything that sinks slightly (including you) is sprung weight. Unsprung weight, on the other hand, is everything else – wheels, tyres, brakes and part of the suspension itself – that *isn't* supported.

Too much unsprung weight is a problem: the more of it there is, the more momentum it has when it moves in reaction to the bike hitting a bump. This momentum has to be controlled by the suspension, giving it more work to do. Unsprung weight also makes the suspension less able to react to bumps quickly, because the extra mass has higher inertia, making it harder to

move. In a perfect world, unsprung weight would be zero. In reality this is impossible, but in practice the figure that matters most is the ratio of sprung to unsprung – the lower the proportion of unsprung, the better.

Telescopic forks
By far the most common type of motorcycle front suspension is the telescopic fork, which is also part of the steering arrangement. The fork is relatively simple in its basic form, each leg consisting of two metal tubes – the moving fork slider and the stationary fork tube. The slider has a slightly larger diameter than the tube, and slides over it. The slider is normally made of aluminium alloy and the fork tube of steel, though various coatings are used to make the sliding motion as smooth as possible.

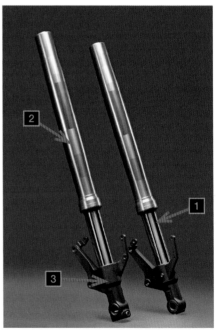

Upside-down forks: 1 Stanchion, 2 Slider, 3 Mounting 'foot'. (Yamaha)

BMW's Telelever front end is an alternative to conventional telescopic forks.
(BMW)

Fork cutaway to show long internal spring. (Kawasaki)

The top of the fork tubes are attached to two triple clamps bolted to the steering head and steering head tube – thus they are an integral part of the steering mechanism. The sliders are mounted at the bottom, bolted to the front wheel's axle.

Inside each fork is a long coil spring, and as the front wheel hits a bump, the slider slides over the fork tube, compressing the spring which absorbs the kinetic energy. The difference between the fork length at rest (with no rider on board) and when fully compressed is referred to in spec sheets as the suspension travel. Off-road bikes will have far more suspension travel than road bikes.

The coil spring may have a progressive rate – that is, it gets stiffer the further it's compressed. Whether progressive or not, the spring rate can be adjusted by altering the 'preload.' This is the small amount of compression on the spring when it is supporting only the weight of the bike with no rider. Increasing the preload has the effect of making the spring stiffer before it begins to react to bumps.

As mentioned earlier, after hitting a bump, a spring without damping would compress, rebound, then continue bouncing up and down. This would make the bike unstable, so hydraulic damping is incorporated into each fork leg. The damper has a sealed rod and piston, with very small passages for the hydraulic fluid to pass through – it's the resistance of the fluid to passing through these passages that provides the damping.

Cartridge forks are a more recent development and offer more damping adjustment. They have different sized oil passages: a low speed (speed of the hydraulic fluid) passage to cope with mild undulations, and medium and high speed passages for bigger bumps.

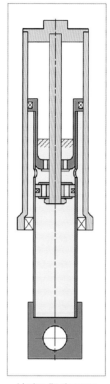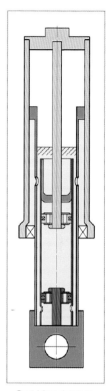

Hydraulic damper inside fork. (Suzuki)

Cartridge damper. (Suzuki)

Some of the passages are opened and closed by one-way valves. Compression and rebound damping are served by different valves, which can be designed to best suit those needs, and allows separate adjustment of compression and rebound damping.

Upside-down forks are just as the name suggests. The outer slider is at the top, fixed by the triple clamps, and the slimmer inner fork tube is at the bottom, located on the front axle. They are stiffer than conventional forks, because the slider is located more rigidly. One variation of the telescopic fork is BMW's Telelever, which uses the forks for guidance only – the single spring/damper unit is located on a

BMW's air damping systems use air instead of oil. (BMW)

Rear shock with damper inside coil spring. (BMW)

swingarm at the steering head. It's a good system that can eliminate fork dive under heavy braking.

Rear suspension
Up until the late 1970s, most motorcycle rear suspension consisted of a double-sided swingarm, pivoting just behind the gearbox and supporting two spring/damper units (shocks). Since then, the single rear shock absorber (sometimes called the monoshock) layout has become dominant, though twin-shock rear ends are still popular on cruisers and some retro bikes. Single-shock systems can use double-sided or single-sided swingarms.

The shock absorber consists of a large coil spring with a hydraulic damper

Single-sided swingarms leave one side of the rear wheel open. (Triumph)

1 Single rear shock (shock absorber),
2 Swingarm. (Yamaha)

Rear shock (shock absorber) with mounting
linkage and adjuster. (Yamaha)

located inside it. One end of the shock is bolted to the frame, the other to the swingarm, though the swingarm connection is often via a series of links. These links can be designed to give a rising rate to the rear shock, especially important for off-road bikes.

As with the telescopic fork, the damper relies on the resistance of hydraulic fluid passing through a small passage to provide the damping. Inside the shock is a piston with precise holes and passages, or oilways, machined into it. The rate at which the fluid passes through these oilways determines the rate at which the piston (and therefore the spring) can move. There is always space for gas (usually air) as well as fluid: the fluid is incompressible, so a fully compressed shock full of fluid would blow the seals.

Again, as with the fork, spring preload is adjustable (usually by a threaded adjuster that bears down on top of the spring), and often the damping is, too. Remote damping and preload adjustment is sometimes provided on touring bikes, to allow quick and convenient suspension adjustment to cope with a passenger and luggage.

Wheels & tyres

Motorcycle wheels do exactly the same job as car wheels – they partly support the weight of the vehicle, cope with braking, acceleration and cornering forces, and provide a mounting point for tyres, brakes and wheel bearings. Wheel design has an effect on how the bike handles. Wheels obviously have to be strong enough to cope with dynamic forces, but weight is important too. The wheel is part of the motorcycle's unsprung weight – that is, weight that has to move *with* the suspension, rather than be supported by it. The heavier the wheel, the slower the suspension responds to uneven surfaces, and the greater the energy required to accelerate and steer the wheel. The ideal wheel, therefore, is both light and strong.

Spoked wheels are strong and still popular. (Harley-Davidson)

Two ball bearings are usually fitted to the wheel axle, and separated by a tubular spacer to prevent side loading on the bearings when the axle is secured. There are two basic types of wheel: spoked and one-piece cast.

Spoked wheels
The spoked wheel is one of the most elegant pieces of engineering ever devised – not to mention rebuildable and very strong. However, they are heavier than some solid wheels, and far more labour-intensive to build, which is why they are restricted to specialist markets.

The spoked wheel consists of three elements: the hub, the spokes and the rim. The hub is hollow and contains either a drum brake, or (more usually, now) the mounting points for a disc brake. The rim is of aluminium alloy – chrome-plated steel is cheaper, but heavy, and has largely been superseded.

But it's the spokes that do much of the wheel's work. These are made of steel for strength, and link the rim to the hub, poking through holes in the rim and secured by a threaded nipple. Spoked wheels have traditionally used tubed tyres, though some manufacturers, notably BMW, have produced spoked wheels that can accept tubeless tyres.

Take a close look at a spoked wheel and you'll see that the spokes aren't mounted radially (ie, at 90 degrees to the hub), but tangentially, with half of them slanting backwards,

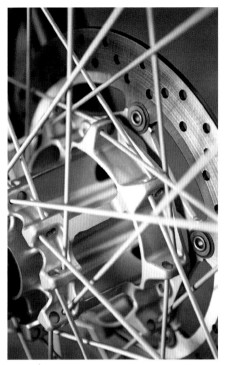

Spokes attach to a hub. (Harley-Davidson)

Cast wheels are strong and simple to mass produce. (Harley-Davidson)

and half forwards. This enables them to cope with braking and acceleration forces, which would quickly cause radial spokes to snap.

All of this only works if the spokes are correctly tensioned, which is why building a spoked wheel is a skilled job. All the spokes must be tensioned evenly (by tightening the nipple) until the wheel runs completely straight and true. Some of the spokes will need retensioning over time. One advantage of the spoked wheel is that, if it suffers crash damage, it can be rebuilt with new spokes and rim, if the hub is undamaged.

Cast wheels
Cast wheels, usually made from aluminium alloy, are now the standard wheel for most road-going bikes. All the same elements as the spoked wheel are present – hub, spokes and rim – doing the same job, but cast as one piece. There are very few spokes, as few as three, but their size and strength mean they don't need to be mounted tangentially; they can, in fact, be used as a styling feature, with no effect on their strength.

Early cast wheels on racing bikes were made of magnesium alloy, but aluminium alloy is used for today's road bike wheels, being cheaper, tougher and just as strong, albeit heavier. But progress never stops in racing, and the latest wheels are constructed of carbon fibre, much lighter even than magnesium, and stronger than aluminium alloy. They're also expensive, though some top-end sports road bikes use them.

Unlike the spoked wheel, no maintenance is needed, though if the cast wheel is involved in an impact, it should be replaced even if there's no visible damage. This is because invisible stress fractures can occur, which weaken the wheel and can lead to sudden failure (though this is very rare). With no spoke holes in the rim, cast wheels can accept tubeless tyres if the rim is of a suitable cross-section, and tubeless tyres are increasingly the dominant type.

Composite wheels, which are rarely seen now, were a sort of hybrid between cast and spoked wheels. The spokes (usually five or six) were of pressed steel or aluminium, and riveted or bolted to the hub and rim. They didn't require tensioning and could use a common hub, with spokes to fit different rim sizes.

One other wheel type is the solid wheel, which is literally solid, like a car wheel. The Harley-Davidson FatBoy is one notable user, but solid wheels bring a weight penalty and make the bike more susceptible to side winds.

Tyres

To the outsider, motorcyclists can appear to be obsessed with tyres, but there's a very good reason why. As well as being safety critical, bike tyres have a far more demanding job than do car or truck tyres. There are only two of them to support the bike's weight and cope with braking, acceleration and cornering forces, and they do all of this with a very small portion of rubber in contact with the road at any one time – the 'contact patch.' That's why motorcycle tyres have a far shorter life than car tyres – 5-6000 miles for a rear tyre is about average.

Fundamental to every motorcycle tyre is the carcass, a layering of plies (synthetic fibre cords, coated in rubber) that gives the tyre its strength. Again, it's a difficult job, as plies have to make the tyre stiff enough to keep it's shape under tremendous forces, but also allow it to flex so that it can follow road imperfections and maximise the contact patch. Traditionally, the plies were laid in alternate diagonal directions, the classic crossply tyre. This made for a nice stiff sidewall, but allowed the tyre to expand at high speed under centrifugal force.

The solution was the radial-ply tyre, and is now almost universal on

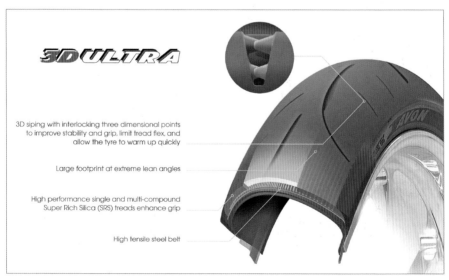

3D ULTRA

3D siping with interlocking three dimensional points to improve stability and grip, limit tread flex, and allow the tyre to warm up quickly

Large footprint at extreme lean angles

High performance single and multi-compound Super Rich Silica (SRS) treads enhance grip

High tensile steel belt

Typical tyre construction. (Cooper-Avon)

modern motorcycles. On a radial tyre, the plies run straight across the tyre at 90 degrees to the tread. Wider, lower profile tyres, with stiffer sidewalls made this possible, bringing a whole raft of advantages over crossply. Radial-ply tyres are lighter, deform less, are less likely to overheat, and offer less rolling resistance. The latest development in radial tyres is the monospiral, which replaces multiple ply belts with a single belt running around the circumference of the tyre.

Like a car tyre, a motorcycle tyre has a reinforced bead on each edge, which keeps it in place on the rim. The tyre may have an inner tube, like a bicycle, but, increasingly, modern bike tyres are tubeless. This necessitates

Modern radial tyres give excellent grip. (Avon)

an airtight rim, but brings advantages – when tubeless tyres puncture, they lose air more gradually.

The tyre tread is made of a synthetic rubber compound, carefully chosen for its balance of grip and wear resistance. A softer compound will grip better but wear faster, so the choice has much to do with the type of bike involved and the sort of use it's likely to see. As ever, the final choice is a compromise, but a dual-compound tyre, with a harder compound in the centre of the tread for straight-running wear resistance, and a softer one on the edge for grip in corners, gives greater versatility.

As with a car tyre, a bike tyre has grooves cut into it to allow surface water to escape – if it didn't have these, the tyre would very soon lose all grip on the tarmac in wet conditions. Tyre pressures are also vital to grip and good handling. It's always best to stick to the manufacturer's recommendations, with extra pressure in the rear tyre to cope with the weight of a passenger and luggage, when needed.

Tyre markings
The average tyre sidewall is covered in markings. Take 180/55ZR17 for example, a very common size.

180 – tyre width in mm

55 – aspect ratio (height of tyre as a percentage of width)

ZR – speed rating, the maximum allowable speed (ZR is 150mph and above)

17 – the wheel diameter, in inches

The load rating appears in brackets after the size/speed markings, and indicates how much weight the tyre can carry – a load rating of 40 = a maximum load of 140kg, 50 = 190kg. Remember, that's not the entire weight of the bike, simply the front or rear load. Tyres may also be marked 'FRONT' or 'REAR' if they have a specific fitment, and have an arrow indicating the direction of rotation. A maximum pressure marking is exactly what it says: *maximum* pressure, not something the tyre should automatically be set to.

Brakes

Motorcycle brakes work on the same principle as any other brake – a pad or shoe is pressed against a disc or drum to slow it down, and therefore slow the motorcycle. Drum brakes are now restricted to the rear wheels of low cost commuters and some smaller off-road bikes, operated by a cable or metal rod. Every other powered two-wheeler uses hydraulic disc brakes – one or two discs for the front wheel, and one disc for the rear. Unlike every other road vehicle (apart from those bikes with linked braking systems – see page 70), these are controlled separately, the front brake by a handlebar lever, and the rear by a foot pedal. Most automatic scooters have two handlebar levers to operate front and rear brakes, like a bicycle.

Hydraulics
A few early disc brakes were cable operated, but hydraulics have become universal because they are the only way to exert sufficient force on the brake pad. Hydraulic fluid cannot be compressed, so pushing a piston at one end of a sealed pipe full of fluid will move a piston at the other end by an equal amount. On a bike, the cylinder for the first piston is the master cylinder, mounted next to the brake lever or pedal, and usually incorporates a fluid reservoir. When the lever or pedal is pushed, this piston pushes fluid down the hydraulic line to the brake caliper, where it forces a second piston (there

may be more than one) through its own cylinder, against the pad that is in turn pushed against the disc.

A question that many people ask is: How does the piston draw back on its own when the brakes are released, as there's no obvious spring to do the job? But there is. There must be a seal between the piston and cylinder, to prevent fluid escaping and air getting in. This is designed to distort slightly as the piston passes through it, so that when you ease off the brake lever and the hydraulic pressure is released, the seal (wanting to return to its original shape) pushes the piston back again. A useful side effect of hydraulic disc brakes is that as the pad wears, the piston must move further to compensate, drawing extra fluid from the reservoir at the lever or pedal. This makes the brake self-adjusting. That's also why the fluid level in the reservoir needs checking, and possibly topping-up, as the pads wear.

The movement of the parts involved in operating a disc brake are tiny – watch the pads as someone else pulls the brake lever, and you can barely

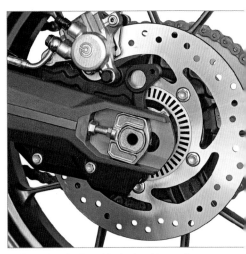

Rear disc brake with single-piston caliper. (Yamaha)

Combined brake master cylinder/reservoir/
brake lever on a Triumph. (Veloce)

detect any movement at all. But disc
brakes are very powerful things, as
they should be, when you think of the
force needed to stop a quarter-tonne
motorcycle travelling at 150mph.

In fact, a very simple hydraulic
system as described above wouldn't
have enough muscle to stop a 150mph
bike. So the force the rider can exert is
multiplied by using a larger piston in the
caliper than in the master cylinder. The
force is also multiplied by using multiple
pistons in the caliper (anything up to six)
and/or a bigger disc.

Cutaway caliper, showing the two pistons.
(Kawasaki)

Calipers

The brake caliper, which holds the
pistons and brake pads, has to be
immensely strong, so as not to distort
under hydraulic pressure. There are
two types of caliper – fixed and floating.
Fixed calipers, sometimes referred to
as opposed piston calipers, are bolted
solidly to the fork leg or swingarm,
and straddle the disc, with a piston on
each side (sometimes two or three).
As pressure is applied, the opposing
pistons move inwards towards the
disc. The inside set of pistons (those
nearest the wheel) are often smaller
than the outer set, giving more uniform
pad wear. Some fixed calipers have a

separate brake pad for each piston, to
minimise deformation of the pad – in
which case the pistons are all the same
size.

The sliding caliper consists of the
caliper itself, and a bracket with pins on
which the caliper can slide. The piston
(again, there may be one, two or three) is
on the outside of the caliper only, while
the inside of the caliper simply cradles
the opposing pad. When the brake is
applied the piston pushes the outside
pad against the disc. At the same time,
the hydraulic pressure pushes the caliper
body along the pins, pulling the inner pad

against the disc, too.

Sliding calipers have some advantages over fixed calipers. With half as many pistons and cylinders, they're cheaper, easier to make, and potentially lighter. Being less bulky on the inside (no piston to accommodate) they suit spoked wheels.

Both types of caliper are vulnerable to corrosion and road dirt, which can cause pistons to stick. If one fixed piston caliper sticks, this leads to uneven braking, and the same effect comes from corrosion or wear in the sliding caliper pins.

We've already mentioned how calipers can house multiple pistons. Two or three small pistons can operate the same pad surface area as one bigger one, but with a smaller (and therefore lighter) disc. Sometimes the multiple pistons are different sizes, which makes the braking more progressive, as smaller pistons move further for each millimetre of movement at the lever or pedal. They push the pad before the bigger ones, giving a progressively stronger effect as lever pressure increases.

The brake discs (or 'rotors') are usually made of stainless steel, drilled with small holes that help dissipate water and assist cooling. A 'floating' disc is mounted on dowels, allowing for better disc centring, and reduced heat transfer to the wheel hub (discs get very hot). Many sports bikes now use 'wave' or 'petal' discs, the outside edge of which is scalloped, rather than following a plain circle. These are said to improve braking performance and feel, by increasing the 'cutting edge' that the pad hits – but they're probably far more relevant on a race track than the ride to work.

Anti-lock brakes

Anti-lock brakes, commonly known as ABS, prevent the brakes from locking. Electronic sensors measure the speed of each wheel and send this information to an electronic control unit (ECU). The ECU then compares the wheels speeds, and if they differ by more than a certain amount (usually about 30%, which indicates an imminent lock-up), sends a message to a pressure modulator that momentarily releases hydraulic pressure to the affected wheel.

The pressure release is only for a split-second, and the modulator will pulse the pressure on and off many times per second. This can sometimes be detected as a pulsing at the brake lever or pedal.

In the early days of ABS, it was an expensive option restricted to top-end touring machines. But it's now much more common, a standard fitting on many big bikes, and a reasonably priced option on some mid-size commuters, as well as sports bikes.

Linked brakes

Since the pioneer days of the early 20th Century, motorcycles have had separate control of front and rear brakes. This requires a certain amount of skill to operate safely, balancing the use the brakes together according to road conditions, and many riders prefer to have individual control for each brake.

Nevertheless, linked systems, in which both brakes are operated by a single pedal or lever, are becoming more popular. Moto Guzzi offered such a system for many years, while Honda and BMW have made this a mainstream option. The Honda dual Combined Braking System (CBS) includes a proportional control valve, that controls the front/rear brake balance – the front/rear balance is also altered according to whether the brake lever or brake pedal is operated.

five

Electrics – the basics

The modern motorcycle has a complex electrical system, with numerous circuits that can include everything from lighting, instrument displays, and anti-lock braking systems, to heated handlebar grips. However, the basics are still the same as when motorcycle electrics were limited to ignition, lights and horn: they are still based around a generator to produce electricity, a battery to store it, and a wiring loom to connect everything up.

How electricity works

Some people find electricity hard to understand, but think of it like water, and it's not so tricky – in fact, some electrical terminology (current, flow) reflects this similarity. Electricity is a flow of electrons through a conductor (the wiring). In order to flow, it must have two things: a complete circuit, from the positive side of a battery to the negative,

Instrument panel is an essential part of the electrics. (Yamaha)

and a potential difference. The potential difference is just like the difference in water pressure created by a pump, causing water to flow. In the case of an electrical circuit, it's the battery that provides this difference. The 'pressure' difference is measured in volts, and the flow, or the current, is measured in amps. The size of the flow depends on the voltage, and the resistance of the wiring to the flow – that's why wiring is made of copper, it's a very good conductor of electricity.

Nowadays, all motorcycle generators are alternators, with outputs growing by the year as manufacturers add more electrically-powered features. The alternator converts mechanical energy into electricity through a process called electromagnetic induction, and consists of the stator (a series of copper wire coils) and a rotor, that rotates around it. The rotor contains magnets, and as these pass over the stator's coils, they pass through the magnetic field and an electrical current is induced in the coils.

So now we have a current, which is heading to the battery for storage, but its flow is controlled by an electronic voltage regulator/rectifier. This does two jobs; first, it converts the alternating current produced by the alternator to a direct current that can be stored by the battery. Second, it protects the battery from being overcharged by dumping excess voltage to earth.

Battery

Batteries have become a hot topic, as the debate over the practicality of electric vehicles gathers pace. The challenge here is to create a battery that is lightweight, compact and with a big enough capacity to power an electric car or two-wheeler for an acceptable range. The electric scooters (and a few e-motorcycles) on the market mostly use lithium-ion batteries, though they still have a relatively limited range.

Things are much simpler for the battery in a petrol (gasoline)-powered bike. The demands are much lower, so the lead-acid type is still dominant, as it's cheap and reliable. Internally, the battery is divided into cells, each of which house a number of alloy plates (alternately positive and negative) immersed in an electrolytic solution, either a liquid or a gel. A chemical reaction between the alloy plates and the electrolyte can work to either store or release electrical energy. Once needing maintenance in the form of topping-up the electrolyte, most batteries are now sealed and maintenance-free.

Electric start

For many years, just about all motorcycles relied on a good healthy swing on the kickstarter to get them fired up. Then, from the late 1960s, the Japanese, led by Honda, began to fit compact electric starters. Now, they're universal on all powered two-wheelers, though some of the 125cc commuters retain a kickstart as well, as an insurance against their smaller batteries losing charge. The starter is basically a generator operating in reverse, with electrical power fed in and converted to mechanical energy. They turn over the engine either by engaging directly with teeth on the flywheel, or through a series of gears, or a chain.

As mentioned at the beginning of this section, there are numerous electrical devices on motorcycles, including engine ancillaries such as the cooling fan and fuel injectors, as well as more luxurious items. All are protected by fuses, so that should a fault occur, the fuse blows – breaking the circuit – to protect the electrical system.

six

Help yourself: keeping your motorcycle working

A lot of riders like to talk about their relationship with their bike, and it's not all hogwash. It sounds trite to say 'look after your bike and it'll look after you,' but it's true, nonetheless. Given regular maintenance and a sympathetic owner, the average modern motorcycle will cover high mileages over many years very reliably.

• Keep an eye and ear open for unusual sounds or vibrations – components rarely fail out of the blue, but after a series of warning signs.
• Keep a full service history. Even if you do the work yourself, it will enable you to keep track of what has been done and what needs doing. It'll also impress a buyer, if you come to sell the bike.
• Servicing can be complicated on modern bikes – even getting access to the sparkplugs, for example – so

you may want to leave most jobs to a professional. But changing the oil and filter is usually quite simple, and it's the most important single job you can do to keep the engine healthy. Very satisfying, too.
• Racing starts, wheelies and stoppies can be fun, but not only do they attract unwanted attention, they also give the clutch, front fork seals, chain, and steering head bearings a very hard time – all will last longer if you don't indulge.
• Keep an eye on your tyres and check the pressures regularly, not forgetting to add pressure to the rear when carrying a pillion and/or heavy luggage. At the same time, turning up the preload will give the rear shock an easier time.
• Look after your bike's drive chain, keeping it clean and well lubed – this should mean less adjustment and a longer life.

seven

Glossary

Bhp
Brake horsepower, a measure of the engine's output, in terms of work done over time, measured at the engine flywheel, before any transmission losses. Some manufacturers and markets now measure power in kW – 1bhp = 0.7457kW

Lb ft
'Pound-foot,' a measure of torque, or the engine's turning effort. As noted on page 14, it's the shape of the torque curve, rather than the peak figure that appears on specification sheets, that has the most relevance to a bike's performance. The metric equivalent to lb ft is Newton Metres (Nm) – 1lb ft = 1.356Nm

Miles per gallon
A measure of how economical a vehicle is, and it's self-explanatory, though many riders prefer 'miles per tankful.' The latter is useful because bikes have smaller fuel tanks than cars, so fuel range is more of an issue. On the other hand, as fuel prices rise, so does interest in mpg rather than mpt.

HT
High tension. Another term for high voltage.

TDC
Top dead centre. The point at which the piston of a cylinder engine is at the highest point of its stroke.

Stoichiometric ratio
In relation to engines, the optimum ratio of air to fuel required for efficient combustion, or 14.7:1

ECU
Engine control unit (also called a PCM or Powertrain Control Module). A computer that controls a number of actuators, based on input from various engine sensors.

ISBN: 978-1-845843-90-8
• Paperback • 21x14.8cm • £12.99* UK/$24.95* USA
• 128 pages • 92 colour and b&w pictures

Also available in eBook format

For more info on Veloce titles, visit our website at www.veloce.co.uk
• email: info@veloce.co.uk • Tel: +44(0)1305 260068
* prices subject to change, p&p extra

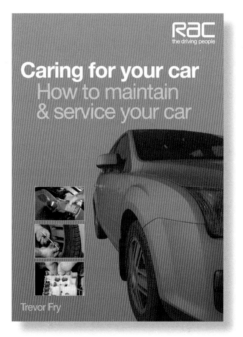

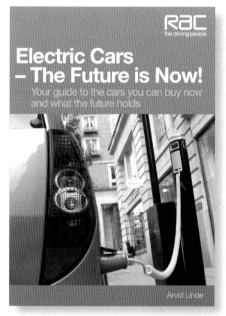

Index